China in Transformation 1900–1949

China in Transformation 1900–1949

Second edition

Colin Mackerras

PEARSON
Longman

Harlow, England • London • New York • Boston • San Francisco • Toronto
Sydney • Tokyo • Singapore • Hong Kong • Seoul • Taipei • New Delhi
Cape Town • Madrid • Mexico City • Amsterdam • Munich • Paris • Milan

PEARSON EDUCATION LIMITED

Edinburgh Gate
Harlow CM20 2JE
United Kingdom
Tel: +44 (0)1279 623623
Fax: +44 (0)1279 431059
Website: www.pearsoned.co.uk

———————————

First edition published 1998
Second edition published 2008

© Pearson Education Limited 2008

The right of Colin Mackerras to be identified as author of this work has been
asserted by him in accordance with the Copyright, Designs and Patents Act 1988.

ISBN: 978-1-4058-4058-3

British Library Cataloguing in Publication Data
A CIP catalogue record for this book can be obtained from the British Library

Library of Congress Cataloging in Publication Data
A CIP catalog record for this book can be obtained from the Library of Congress

10 9 8 7 6 5 4 3 2 1
11 10 09 08

Set in 10/13.5pt Berkeley Book by 35
Printed and bound in Malaysia (CTP-VVP)

The publisher's policy is to use paper manufactured from sustainable forests.

Introduction to the series

History is a narrative constructed by historians from traces left by the past. Historical enquiry is often driven by contemporary issues and, in consequence, historical narratives are constantly reconsidered, reconstructed and reshaped. The fact that different historians have different perspectives on issues means that there is also often controversy and no universally agreed version of past events. *Seminar Studies in History* was designed to bridge the gap between current research and debate, and the broad, popular general surveys that often date rapidly.

The volumes in the series are written by historians who are not only familiar with the latest research and current debates concerning their topic, but who have themselves contributed to our understanding of the subject. The books are intended to provide the reader with a clear introduction to a major topic in history. They provide both a narrative of events and a critical analysis of contemporary interpretations. They include the kinds of tools generally omitted from specialist monographs: a chronology of events, a glossary of terms and brief biographies of 'who's who'. They also include bibliographical essays in order to guide students to the literature on various aspects of the subject. Students and teachers alike will find that the selection of documents will stimulate discussion and offer insight into the raw materials used by historians in their attempt to understand the past.

Clive Emsley and Gordon Martel
Series Editors

Contents

PART FIVE   DOCUMENTS

Preface

This book is designed for student use, although its author hopes that any person interested in China in the first half of the twentieth century may find it useful. It aims to give an accurate description of how China developed in that period against the background of a framework encompassing certain major themes. Most of the chapters are chronological, but several take up particular topics of importance, including the student movement, education, and aspects of social and cultural change over the half-century of focus.

The book follows the style of the series *Seminar Studies in History*. The documents given in Part Five are chosen to explain and enhance the interest of the text. References to the documents again follow the style of the series.

The system of romanization adopted here is the *pinyin*. This is now in universal currency in the People's Republic of China for publications in languages using the Roman script. It is also followed today in most scholarly work in countries with languages using Roman letters. Exceptions are made for Sun Yat-sen and Chiang Kai-shek, since those two names are widely known in the forms given, which are not *pinyin*. In Part Five, the original romanizations are retained where the documents themselves are in English, but, except for Sun Yat-sen and Chiang Kai-shek, *pinyin* is given in square brackets where it differs.

This book is based on a course called 'China in Transformation, 1900–1949' which the author taught at Griffith University, Brisbane, for several years, and which was established and taught for many years there by Professor Edmund Fung before he took up a Chair at the University of Western Sydney. I wish to thank both Professor Fung and those students who took the subject. Both have given me great inspiration and shared ideas concerning this fascinating and significant period. However, responsibility for the book, and in particular for its deficiencies, lies entirely with the author.

Publisher's acknowledgements

We are grateful to the following for permission to reproduce copyright material:

Plates 1 and 5: Corbis; Plate 3: Alamy; Plate 4: Art Archive; Plate 8: Getty Images.

Maps 1 and 2 from Hsü, Immanuel C. Y., *The Rise of Modern China*, 5th edn, Oxford University Press, New York, 1995. By permission of Oxford University Press, Inc.

In some instances we have been unable to trace the owners of copyright material, and we would appreciate any information that would enable us to do so.

Chronology

1900

Summer   The Boxer Rebellion, including a siege of the legations of the powers.

14 August   Allied troops of eight powers, seven Western and Japan, enter Beijing and lift the siege of the legations.

1901

7 September   The Boxer Protocol, under which China agrees to pay an enormous indemnity to the powers for the Boxer Rebellion.

1904

8 February   The Russo-Japanese War begins. China declared neutrality (12 February), but the war was fought mainly on Chinese soil.

1905

2 September   An imperial decree abolishes the traditional examination system.

5 September   The signature of the Treaty of Portsmouth ends the Russo-Japanese War, giving formerly Russian interests in Manchuria to Japan.

1908

27 August   The court accepts a draft constitution providing for a constitutional monarchy and a parliament.

14 November   Death of the Guangxu Emperor, followed by that of the Empress Dowager Cixi the next day.

1909

5 February   Preliminary local elections begin, selecting delegates for provincial assemblies, which meet later in the year.

1911

10 October   The Wuchang uprising sparks the collapse of the Qing dynasty: the 1911 Revolution.

1912

1 January   Official proclamation of the Republic of China (ROC). Sun Yat-sen becomes provisional ROC president.

12 February   Formal abdication of the Qing Emperor.

15 February   Yuan Shikai appointed provisional ROC president in place of Sun Yat-sen.

25 August   The Nationalist Party founded, with Sun Yat-sen as chairman.

1913

July–September   The 'Second Revolution' consolidates Yuan Shikai's power.

6 October   The National Assembly formally elects Yuan Shikai as ROC president.

1914

10 January   Yuan Shikai suspends the National Assembly.

6 August   Yuan Shikai declares China neutral in the First World War.

1915

26 January   Japan presents its Twenty-one Demands to China.

25 May   China and Japan sign treaties based on the Twenty-one Demands.

1916

6 June   Yuan Shikai dies, having tried unsuccessfully to restore the monarchy, with himself as emperor.

1917

1 July   The last Qing Emperor is restored to the throne but forced to abdicate again later the same month.

14 August   China declares war on Germany and Austria-Hungary.

10 September   Sun Yat-sen establishes the Republic of China (ROC) Military Government in Guangzhou.

6 October   War breaks out between the Beijing and Guangzhou governments.

1918

November   The war between the Beijing and Guangzhou governments ends with a
           ceasefire.

1919

30 April   At the Paris Peace Conference, which followed the end of the First World
           War, the major powers accept a demand put forward by Japan for the
           transfer of all previous German interests in Shandong Province.

4 May   Major student demonstrations against China's treatment at the Paris Peace
           Conference begin – the May Fourth Movement.

1920

29 June   China joins the League of Nations.

16 December   Earthquakes shake Gansu and elsewhere in north China, with several
           hundred thousand casualties.

1921

5 May   Sun Yat-sen assumes the position of extraordinary president of the ROC,
           with the capital in Guangzhou, his wish being to carry out a 'Northern
           Expedition' to reunite the country.

July   First Congress of the Chinese Communist Party (CCP), mainly in Shanghai.

1922

3 February   Sun Yat-sen orders that the Northern Expedition be launched to reunite the
           country.

9 August   Sun Yat-sen flees Guangzhou, the Northern Expedition having been
           aborted due to a conflict between Sun and Guangdong warlord governor
           Chen Jiongming.

1 November   A presidential mandate promulgates a new American-influenced education
           system.

1923

26 January   Joint communique by Sun Yat-sen and Soviet representative Adolf Joffe.

7 February   A major workers' strike on the Beijing–Hankou railway is put down by the
           army, and over thirty workers are shot dead.

17 March   Having become generalissimo of a new Guangzhou government on
           2 March, Sun Yat-sen appoints Chiang Kai-shek as Guangzhou
           government chief-of-staff.

1924

20–30 January The First Congress of the Nationalist Party in Guangzhou.

31 May The Sino-Soviet Agreement, by which China recognizes the Soviet Union, with the latter renouncing extraterritoriality in China.

26 November The Mongolian People's Republic adopts a constitution proclaiming Mongolia independent of China.

1925

12 March Death of Sun Yat-sen in Beijing.

30 May A demonstration in Shanghai is fired on by British police, who kill, wound and arrest many Chinese students, leading on to strikes, demonstrations and disturbances aimed against the British and other authorities: the May Thirtieth Movement.

1 July Formal establishment of the National Government of the Republic of China (ROC) in Guangzhou.

1926

1–19 January Second Congress of the Nationalist Party held in Guangzhou.

20 March The *Zhongshan* Incident: Chiang Kai-shek arrests Li Zhilong, a CCP member and captain of the *SS Zhongshan*, thus beginning his campaign against the CCP.

1 July Chiang Kai-shek orders that the Northern Expedition begin, with the aim of reuniting the whole country.

1927

24 March National Revolutionary Army troops take Nanjing on their Northern Expedition.

12 April Chiang Kai-shek carries out an anti-Communist coup in Shanghai and begins large-scale slaughter of Communists.

18 April Nanjing becomes the capital of the National Government.

1 August A CCP-led uprising in Nanchang, capital of Jiangxi Province, begins. Although suppressed by 5 August, the CCP still celebrates 1 August as 'Army Day' because of this uprising.

11–13 December A CCP-led uprising in Guangzhou is suppressed: the Canton Commune.

14 December China's National Government breaks off diplomatic relations with the Soviet Union.

1928

6 June   The Northern Expedition takes Beijing, the name of which is changed to Beiping on 28 June. (Since Nanjing means literally 'southern capital' and Beijing 'northern capital', the latter city was called Beiping, literally 'northern peace', while Nanjing remained the capital.)

10 October   Chiang Kai-shek's formal inauguration as chairman of the National Government.

29 December   Manchurian warlord Zhang Xueliang submits to Chiang Kai-shek, signalling the reunification of China under Chiang Kai-shek.

1929

15–28 March   Third National Party Congress in Nanjing, with a Central Executive Committee (including Chiang Kai-shek, Hu Hanmin and Wang Jingwei) elected on 27 March.

1930

All year   The number dying of starvation from the great drought-famine of 1928–30 reaches many millions.

1 March   Wang Jingwei is expelled from the Nationalist Party.

1 May   Chiang Kai-shek declares war against warlords Yan Xishan and Feng Yuxiang, winning the war in October the same year.

1931

28 July   The Yangzi River bursts its banks in Hankou, causing catastrophic flooding.

18 September   The Mukden Incident: Japanese troops occupy a Chinese barracks near Shenyang (Mukden), leading on to the conquest of all Manchuria (northeast China) by the end of the year.

7 November   The CCP establishes its Chinese Soviet Republic, with the capital in Ruijin, Jiangxi Province. Mao Zedong is appointed chairman of the government on 27 November.

1932

9 March   The Japanese-sponsored state of Manchukoku is formally set up in northeast China, with its capital in Changchun, and Qing Emperor Puyi is inaugurated as chief executive.

12 December   China and the Soviet Union announce resumption of diplomatic relations.

1933

24 February The League of Nations Assembly resolves that its members will refuse to recognize Manchukoku, prompting Japan to withdraw from the League on 27 March.

31 May Chinese and Japanese representatives sign the Tanggu Truce, under which China relinquishes control of the northeast provinces to Japan.

1934

Most serious combination of drought and flood for several decades.

19 February Chiang Kai-shek launches the New Life Movement, aimed at promoting Confucian virtues.

1 March The last Qing Emperor Puyi ascends the throne in Changchun as Emperor of Manchukoku.

16 October Mao Zedong and Zhu De lead the Red Army's First Front Army west, abandoning the capital of the Chinese Soviet Republic Ruijin and beginning the Long March.

10 November Chiang Kai-shek's troops enter Ruijin.

1935

20 October The Long March ends in Wuqizhen, northern Shaanxi.

28 October Japanese Foreign Minister Hirota Koki announces his Three Principles advocating a Japan-China-Manchukoku Axis against communism and for the development of north China.

9 December Student demonstrations protesting against Japanese imperialism and government failure to resist it begin in Beiping: the December Ninth Movement.

1936

12 December The Xi'an Incident: Chiang Kai-shek's generals Yang Hucheng and Zhang Xueliang place him under house arrest to demand effective resistance against Japan and an end to civil war.

Mid–late December The CCP moves its headquarters to Yan'an, northern Shaanxi.

25 December Chiang Kai-shek is released on his acknowledgment of the need for resistance to Japan.

1937

7 July The Marco Polo Bridge Incident sparks the Sino-Japanese War. Japanese troops attack Chinese near the Lugou (Marco Polo) Bridge outside Beiping.

13 December	Having occupied Nanjing, Japanese troops begin the Nanjing Massacre, killing at least 100,000 people.

1938

7 June	Chinese troops burst the dykes of the Yellow River near Zhengzhou, Henan Province, to prevent Japanese troops from their southward advance, causing flooding so severe as to cause the river to change course.
21 October	Guangzhou falls to the Japanese.
Mid-November	Fire in Changsha, capital of Hunan Province, kills many people and causes great devastation. The fire, which lasted several days, had been deliberately lit in the false belief that the Japanese had occupied the city.

1939

29 September– *6 October*	China wins the first battle for the city of Changsha.

1940

30 March	A pro-Japanese government is formally established in Nanjing, with Wang Jingwei as its head.
30 November	Japan recognizes Wang Jingwei's regime, the two signing a treaty leaving the main power with Japan.

1941

4–15 January	The Southern Anhui Incident: Nationalist troops inflict serious damage on the CCP's New Fourth Army, the effect being to end the united front between the two parties.
1 July	Germany and Italy formally recognize Wang Jingwei's government. Chiang Kai-shek breaks off diplomatic relations with both countries the next day.
8 October	The Second Battle of Changsha ends with a victory for China.
9 December	The National Government declares war against Japan, Germany and Italy, following Japan's attack on Pearl Harbor on 7 December.
25 December	Hong Kong occupied by Japan.

1942

1 January	China signs the United Nations Declaration.
15 January	The Third Battle of Changsha ends with a victory for China.

| 4 March | US General Joseph Stilwell becomes chief-of-staff of the China war theatre. |
| 2 June | China and the USA reach the Sino-US Lend-Lease Agreement. |

1943

All year	Catastrophic drought-famine kills millions, especially in Henan Province.
11 January	China signs treaties with the USA and Britain by which extraterritoriality is abolished.
March	Mao Zedong becomes chairman of the Politburo of the CCP Central Committee.
10 March	*China's Destiny* by Chiang Kai-shek is published in Chongqing.
1 December	The Cairo Conference, which Chiang Kai-shek had attended, issues the Cairo Declaration, one part declaring the Manchuria and Taiwan will be returned to China with victory against Japan.

1944

18 April	Japan begins its general offensive from north to south China, the Transcontinental Offensive, giving Japan effective control over an unbroken railway from Korea to Vietnam by November.
18 June	Changsha falls to Japanese troops of the Transcontinental Offensive.
July	China takes part in the United Nations Monetary and Financial Conference held at Bretton Woods in the USA, with China named one of the directors of the proposed World Bank on 19 July.
10 November	Death of Wang Jingwei in Japan.

1945

4–11 February	The Yalta Conference.
26 June	China and other nations sign the United Nations Charter in San Francisco.
9 August	Soviet troops enter northeast China.
14 August	China and the Soviet Union sign their Treaty of Friendship and Alliance in Moscow.
9 September	The Japanese formally surrender in the China theatre.
25 November	Students of the Southwest Associated University in Kunming, capital of Yunnan, begin demonstrations in protest against the civil war policies of the Chiang Kai-shek government.

1946

5 May Chiang Kai-shek formally transfers his capital back to Nanjing.

26 June Chiang Kai-shek's troops launch an offensive against CCP-held areas in central China, signalling the outbreak of civil war.

25 December Adoption of the ROC constitution.

1947

15 March Completion of repair work on the Yellow River dykes, the Yellow River consequently reverting to its pre-1938 course.

19 March Chiang Kai-shek's troops retake Yan'an.

4 May Beginning of a new student–worker movement in Shanghai, protesting against hunger, inflation and civil war. The movement later spreads to other major cities.

13 May CCP troops begin an offensive in northeast China.

1948

2 April The US Congress passes the China Aid Act, granting US$338 million to China.

19 August Chiang Kai-shek attempts, unsuccessfully, to control runaway inflation through the promulgation of the Financial and Economic Emergency Discipline Regulations.

2 November CCP troops capture Shenyang, signalling their total victory in northeast China.

1949

31 January Beiping falls to CCP troops.

23 April Chiang Kai-shek's capital Nanjing falls to CCP troops.

27 May Shanghai falls to CCP troops.

1 October The People's Republic of China is formally established, with Mao Zedong as chairman of the Central People's Government and Zhou Enlai as premier.

Who's who

Ba Jin (pen-name of Li Yaotang, 1904–2005): One of the leading Chinese novelists of the twentieth century. His best work was written in the 1930s, notably a tragic trilogy about a declining high-class but old-fashioned family. The first novel of the trilogy, *Family* (*Jia*), was completed in 1931 and is among the best and most famous novels of twentieth-century China.

Cao Yu (pen-name of Wan Jiabao, 1910–96): Often dubbed 'China's Shakespeare', he is regarded as the best dramatist of the 'spoken drama', a new form of theatre introduced into China in 1907. Cao Yu's best plays date from the 1930s, his masterpiece being *Thunderstorm* (*Leiyu*), which was published in 1934 and premiered in 1935.

Chen Duxiu (1879–1942): Major progressive thinker and leader of the New Culture Movement. In 1915 Chen founded and edited *Youth Magazine* (*Qingnian zazhi*), later renamed *New Youth* (*Xin qingnian*), the main progressive mouthpiece of the movement. Chen was the leader of those who founded the Chinese Communist Party in May 1920 and was elected secretary-general at its First Congress in 1921, being removed from the position in 1927. Imprisoned by the Nationalist Party government in 1932, he was released on the outbreak of the War Against Japan.

Chiang Kai-shek (1887–1975): Leader of the Nationalist Party government from 1927 until its defeat by the Chinese Communist Party forces in 1949. He led the Northern Expedition of 1927–8, which more or less united China under his rule. His government dates from April 1927 when he carried out a major coup against the Communists in Shanghai, shortly after setting up his capital in Nanjing. He was kidnapped at the end of 1936 by one of his own subordinates, Zhang Xueliang, who aimed to force him to resist Japanese occupation. Though he was acknowledged thereafter as a leader against the Japanese during the war from 1937 to 1945, his government became more and more corrupt and he was defeated in 1949, taking refuge in Taiwan.

Empress Dowager Cixi (1835–1908): Aunt of the Guangxu Emperor, and the effective ruler of China from the early 1860s until her death, though she never rose to the top position of emperor. Highly conservative in her thinking, she strongly opposed the Reform Movement of 1898, but still presided over some important changes in Chinese politics and society after the Boxer Rebellion of 1900.

Guangxu Emperor (1871–1908): Ruled as Chinese emperor from 1875 to his death. He was the nephew of the Empress Dowager Cixi, who used her power to put him on the throne against the rules of succession. Under the influence of reformers Kang Youwei and Liang Qichao, he carried out the Hundred Days' Reform in 1898, instigating thorough-going changes in China's political, social and economic system. Empress Dowager Cixi had him put under house arrest to counter the changes, but most of them came into effect anyway, following the Boxer Rebellion of 1900.

Jiang Jieshi. See Chiang Kai-shek.

Liang Qichao (1873–1929): Leading thinker of the late Qing and Republican period. A major leader, along with Kang Youwei (1858–1927), of the 1898 Hundred Days' Reform, he fled to Japan after its failure, becoming an opponent of Sun Yat-sen. When the Republic was founded in 1912, he became a member of Parliament and accepted several positions under Yuan Shikai, but opposed the latter's monarchist attempts. He retired from political life in 1918, devoting himself to writing, teaching and travel.

Lu Xun (pen-name of Zhou Shuren, 1881–1936): Twentieth-century China's most famous writer. He was noted especially for his socially satiric short stories, the best known being 'The True Story of A Q' ('A Q zhengzhuan'), written between December 1921 and February 1922. Very left-wing in his sympathies, he won fulsome praise from Mao Zedong.

Mao Zedong (1893–1976): Leader of the Chinese Communist Party from January 1935 until his death. He led the famous Long March of 1934–5, thereby saving the Communist forces from total defeat, eventually defeating Chiang Kai-shek in 1949. Though his reputation has suffered greatly in recent decades, he did succeed in setting up the People's Republic of China, one of the few Communist-Party led states to survive into the twenty-first century.

Mei Lanfang (1894–1961): The most famous and probably twentieth-century China's greatest actor and exponent of China's main traditional drama genre *Jingju* (Peking Opera). He was unrivalled in the male *dan* roles, meaning the parts of women played by men. He was also the first prominent Chinese actor to perform abroad, visiting countries such as Japan, the Soviet Union and the USA.

Song Meiling (1897–2003): The youngest of the famous Song sisters and wife of Chiang Kai-shek. She contributed to raising the status of women during the Republican period and was a very strong and articulate advocate for Nationalist China in the USA, where she lived for several decades after Chiang's death.

Song Qingling (1892–1981): The second of the famous three Song sisters and wife of Sun Yat-sen. American educated, she became Sun's secretary in Japan and married him in 1914. After Sun's death she became identified with the left wing and was a figure of suspicion to the government of Chiang Kai-shek (her brother-in-law). She remained prominent in China under the People's Republic.

Sun Yat-sen (1866–1925): Revolutionary and first president of the Republic of China, sometimes known as 'father of the nation' (*guofu*). Sun's first term as president was short and unsuccessful, but he later set up a southern government based in Guangzhou. There he reorganized the Nationalist Party (Guomindang), and its First Congress was held in January 1924 in Guangzhou. Sun Yat-sen did not live to see his dream of national reunification realized, but his three principles of the people (nationalism, democracy and people's livelihood) became the Nationalist Party's official doctrine.

Wang Jingwei (1883–1944): Major Nationalist Party leader, but also collaborator with the Japanese. A foremost supporter of Sun Yat-sen, he aspired to succeed Sun as head of the Nationalist Party and opposed the victor Chiang Kai-shek to the end. Regarded as the leader of the left wing of the Nationalist Party, he remained active within the party. In 1940 he decided to collaborate with the Japanese and was installed at the head of a pro-Japanese government with its capital in Nanjing.

Yuan Shikai (1859–1916): President of the Republic of China. Originally a general and high-ranking official under the Qing dynasty, he was instrumental in forcing the last Qing Emperor, Puyi (1906–67), to abdicate, then took over the presidency from Sun Yat-sen in February 1912. Suppressing all democratic trends, he led an unpopular movement to make himself emperor, but died before he could be forced from power.

Zhang Xueliang (1901–2001): Son of northeast Chinese warlord Zhang Zuolin, whom he succeeded on his father's death in mid-1928. In December

1928 Zhang Xueliang submitted to Chiang Kai-shek, signalling the reunification of China on the Northern Expedition's completion, but then kidnapped him in 1936 to force him to resist Japan. Chiang agreed to the demand but immediately arrested Zhang Xueliang, who spent decades under house arrest, mostly in Taiwan, but settled in Hawai'i in 1994.

Glossary

Boxer Rebellion: A popular rebellion that reached its climax with a siege of the foreign legations in the summer of 1900, provoking an invasion by the world's eight major powers.

Chinese Communist Party (CCP): *Zhongguo Gongchan dang*, the ruling party in China since 1949, but playing an important political role in much of the period after its birth in 1920.

Chinese Soviet Republic: Also known as the Jiangxi Soviet, this was a state established in November 1931 with its capital in Ruijin, Jiangxi Province. It lasted until October 1934, when it was conquered by Nationalist Party troops.

Chinese United League: *Tongmeng hui*, the revolutionary group set up by Sun Yat-sen in 1905 in Tokyo.

Democracy (in Sun's three principles): *Minquan zhuyi*.

Hundred Days' Reform: The name given to the reform period from 11 June to 21 September 1898, when the Qing Emperor promoted policies of reform.

May Fourth Movement: *Wusi yundong*, the process of intellectual, cultural and social revolution in China. The centerpiece event was a major demonstration on 4 May 1919: the May Fourth Incident.

Nanjing decade: The ten years from Nanjing's establishment as the capital of Chiang Kai-shek's National Government to the outbreak of the War Against Japan: 1927–37.

National Revolutionary Army (NRA): The name of Chiang Kai-shek's army in his Northern Expedition, formed in 1925.

Nationalism (in Sun's three principles): *Minzu zhuyi*.

Nationalist Party: *Guomindang*, the ruling party of China from 1927 to 1949.

New Culture Movement: *Xin wenhua yundong*, see May Fourth Movement.

Northern Expedition: The military expedition sent north from Guangzhou to unite the country. The main and successful Northern Expedition was led by Chiang Kai-shek from 1926 to 1928.

Peking Opera: Known nowadays as *jingju* in Chinese, this is the most famous and perhaps most developed of China's traditional theatre genres and probably the nearest to a Chinese national theatre.

People's Liberation Army: *Renmin jiefang jun*, the name given to the CCP's forces from 1 May 1946.

People's livelihood (in Sun's three principles): *Minsheng zhuyi*.

Qing dynasty: The ruling dynasty of China from 1644 to 1911. It is also sometimes called the Manchu dynasty, because the ruling family belonged to the Manchu nationality.

Rectification Movement: A campaign orchestrated by Mao Zedong in the early 1940s in Yan'an and surrounding CCP-controlled areas aimed at imposing his own authority and his brand of Marxism-Leninism on the CCP.

Son of heaven: *Tianzi*, the title given to the Chinese emperor.

Spoken drama: *Huaju*, modern or Western-style drama, in which the spoken word is primary.

Three principles of the people: *Sanmin zhuyi*, Sun Yat-sen's basic philosophy of nationalism, democracy and people's livelihood.

Warlord: *Junfa*, one who commanded a personal army, acting more or less independently.

Xi'an Incident: The kidnap of Chiang Kai-shek in December 1936 to force him to resist Japan.

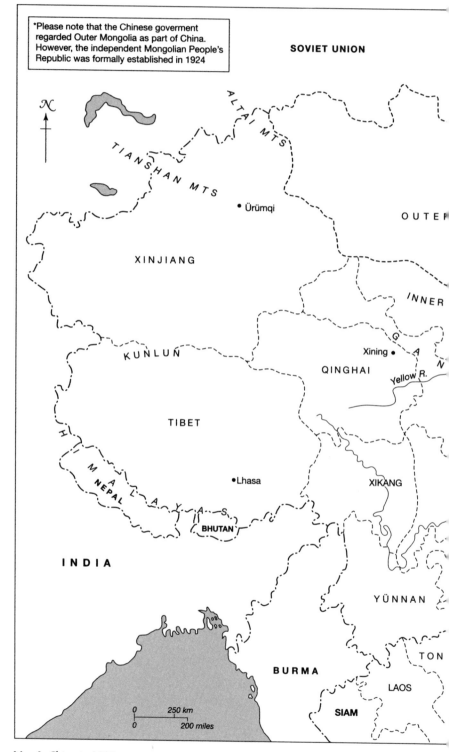

Map 1 China in 1930

Source: Hsü, Immanuel C. Y., *The Rise of Modern China*, 5th edn, Oxford University Press, New York, 1995. Reproduced with permission from Oxford University Press, Inc.

Map 2 The Long March
Source: Hsü, Immanuel C. Y., *The Rise of Modern China*, 5th edn, Oxford University Press, New York, 1995. Reproduced with permission from Oxford University Press, Inc.

Part 1

INTRODUCTION

1

Introduction, Framework and Definitions

The first half of the twentieth century was not a happy period for China. It began with the disastrous **Boxer Rebellion** (1900), which saw the country invaded by the world's eight greatest powers, followed by an extremely humiliating 'protocol' the next year. It ended with the victory of the **Chinese Communist Party** (CCP), after a long period of **warlord** rule, Japanese invasion and civil war.

Historians nowadays are more conscious of the continuities in modern China than was once the case. In particular, the CCP's victory, and hence the year 1949, no longer seems quite as crucial in China's overall history as it once did. Yet both the Boxer Rebellion and the CCP's victory are quite important enough to justify them as boundaries for a book such as this.

The first half of the twentieth century was a period of great importance for China. It witnessed achievements in cultural, social, economic and even political respects. In contrast to several other great pre-twentieth-century empires (such as the Hapsburg and Ottoman), China held together politically, more or less. This was a period when modernization became accepted as an ideal by governments. It saw the blossoming of nationalism to form a powerful political and social force. It saw great reforms at least attempted, albeit haltingly, in several major fields, including education and the status of the peasantry, youth and women. Above all, this period saw the continuation and climax of a revolutionary process that had begun in the middle of the nineteenth century. For all the conservatism and corruption of the Chinese elite, this was a period of enormous and deep-seated change – hence the title of this book, *China in Transformation*.

Boxer Rebellion: A popular rebellion that reached its climax with a siege of the foreign legations in the summer of 1900, provoking an invasion by the world's eight major powers.

Chinese Communist Party (CCP): *Zhongguo Gongchan dang*, the ruling party in China since 1949, but playing an important political role in much of the period after its birth in 1920.

Warlord: *Junfa*, one who commanded a personal army, acting more or less independently.

THEMES IN CHINESE HISTORY, 1900–49

In his introduction to the *Cambridge History* of Republican China, the distinguished historian of China, John King Fairbank (1907–91), placed his focus for treatment of the period on civil war, revolution, invasion and foreign influence, accompanied by 'change and growth in the economic, social, intellectual and cultural spheres' **[Doc. 1, p. 118]**. His view forms part of the theoretical framework of the present book. But, in addition, the concepts of nationalism and modernization are of crucial importance in understanding the period.

The basic framework revolves around four basic tensions. In summary form, these are:

- revolution, reform, change and reaction;
- nationalism and imperialism;
- modernization and tradition;
- foreign impact and internal dynamic.

These tensions, or dichotomies, are related to each other, although they are also quite distinct and separate. Like much historical debate, they involve judgements over who should receive credit and blame for the actions they take and the policies they follow. What influences such value judgements will depend on the sympathies of the observer, as well as the time and place of making them. The intensity of political debate, disagreement and conflict in the first half of the twentieth century in China was so great that political sympathies – towards imperialism, Chinese or Asian nationalism, socialism or communism – create an inevitable impact on the attitudes that an observer will adopt towards the events and trends of China in the period of focus, and towards the policies, ideas and actions of such notable personalities as **Sun Yat-sen**, **Yuan Shikai**, **Chiang Kai-shek**, **Mao Zedong** and **Wang Jingwei**.

Apart from political sympathy, the time and place in which an observer lives cannot help but influence the attitudes adopted towards historical events. An English person in the early twenty-first century is likely to view matters very differently from one in the 1950s, simply because concerns and priorities at the two times were different. And in addition, the history of the intervening decades will certainly have something to tell us about that of the first half of the twentieth century. And as for place, somebody living in Japan is likely to see things differently from the resident of France or Australia, simply because culture, attitudes and values are influenced by national surroundings and events. The globalization that has gathered momentum in the late years of the twentieth century naturally creates its own impact, and in general towards a convergence of opinion. But in the twenty-first century, there is no sign at all that national differences of attitude are disappearing, let alone divergences of political sympathy. And the likelihood is that the significance of the chronological standpoint will persist. It will be surprising indeed if a German of the year 2020 adopts the same attitudes and priorities in judging Chinese history from 1900 to 1949 as a conational at the end of the twentieth century.

REVOLUTION, REFORM, CHANGE AND REACTION

There were several revolutions in China in the first half of the twentieth century. The Revolution of 1911 overthrew the **Qing dynasty** (established in 1644) and, even more importantly, the Chinese monarchy that had lasted for thousands of years. Subsequent attempts to restore the monarchy in China have all proved only temporary or disastrous failures, and in the early twenty-first century it looks as though the republican system in China will survive. The 1911 Revolution was consequently an event of the utmost importance, signalling very dramatic change. The Revolution of 1949 was the one that brought the CCP to power. In terms of the extent of political, economic and social change it wrought, it was an even more significant revolution than its 1911 predecessor. However, in the way it played itself out after its triumph in 1949, it is beyond the scope of the present book.

Apart from these two, there is a range of other series of events that are sometimes described as revolutions. These include the Boxer Rebellion of 1900, the 'Second Revolution' of 1913, the May Fourth Movement of 1919, and the Nationalist Revolution of 1925–7. And there are also revolutions in the field of culture, economy or society, a particularly significant one for China in the first half of the twentieth century being the rural revolution.

These various revolutions have provoked reactions, often amounting to intense hostility. Yet the implications of terms like revolution or revolutionary sometimes depend on the user. Some of China's most significant twentieth-century political leaders regarded themselves as revolutionaries, but were seen as symbols of reaction by their enemies. The most prominent illustrative example was Chiang Kai-shek, who used the term 'Nationalist Revolution' enthusiastically but whom the CCP regarded as an arch-reactionary.

What, then, does the term revolution mean in the context of China in the first half of the twentieth century? *The International Encyclopedia of the Social Sciences* defines a revolution as 'a radical change in the system of government' often involving 'the infringement of prevailing constitutional arrangements

Mao Zedong (1893–1976): Leader of the Chinese Communist Party from January 1935 until his death. Led the famous Long March of 1934–5, saving the Communist forces from total defeat, eventually defeating Chiang Kai-shek in 1949. Set up the People's Republic of China, one of the few Communist-Party led states to survive into the twenty-first century.

Wang Jingwei (1883–1944): Supported Sun Yat-sen and aspired to succeed him as head of the Nationalist Party. Opposed the victor Chiang Kai-shek to the end and was regarded as the leader of the left wing of the party. In 1940 he collaborated with the Japanese and was installed as head of a pro-Japanese government in Nanjing.

Qing dynasty: The ruling dynasty of China from 1644 to 1911. It is also sometimes called the Manchu dynasty, because the ruling family belonged to the Manchu nationality.

and the use of force' (Sills, 1968: XIII, 501). A particularly famous Chinese definition is that of Mao Zedong (1965: I, 28), who wrote in March 1927 that 'a revolution is an insurrection, an act of violence whereby one class over-throws another'.

A political revolution typically involves not merely the overthrow of the government but of the system itself. The essence of a revolution is radical change, which is usually implemented rapidly and with violence. While there is argument over whether a revolution really needs violence to make the term appropriate – the encyclopedia definition refers not to violence but to force – the realities of twentieth-century Chinese history make it reason-able to define a revolution in that context as 'a movement involving violence which brings about radical, and probably rapid, change'. Mao's suggestion that part of a revolution is the overthrow of one class by another is obviously influenced by the Marxist idea of class struggle. While it is very definitely applicable to his own revolution, it is too narrow for the general purposes of this book.

The terms reform and reaction, both important for the topic of this book, carry implications very different from revolution. By comparison with a revolution, a process of reform involves more gradual, less deep-seated and much less violent, or even totally non-violent, change. The antithesis of revolution is not reform, but reaction, which generally sets itself against everything revolutionaries wish to achieve.

Nationalist Party: *Guomindang*, the ruling party of China from 1927 to 1949.

Liang Qichao (1873–1929): Leading thinker of the late Qing and Republican period. A major leader of the 1898 Hundred Days' Reform, he fled to Japan after its failure, becoming an opponent of Sun Yat-sen. At the Repulic's foundation in 1912, he joined Parliament and accepted several posi-tions under Yuan Shikai, but opposed his mon-archist attempts. He retired in 1918.

Three principles of the people: *Sanmin zhuyi,* Sun Yat-sen's basic phi-losophy of nationalism, democracy and people's livelihood.

NATIONALISM AND IMPERIALISM

The significance of the term nationalism (*minzu zhuyi*) in Chinese history from 1900 to 1949 is obvious from the name that the most dominant polit-ical party of the period gave itself: the **Nationalist Party**. It obsessed influential thinkers such as **Liang Qichao [Doc. 7, p. 122]** and political leaders like Sun Yat-sen, who made it the first, and most important, of his **three principles of the people [Doc. 15, p. 128]**. Nationalism was a core component of the succession of student movements occurring over the three decades from 1919 to 1949. Although CCP leaders never spoke of national-ism, they certainly espoused the related concept of patriotism and were in fact nationalist in their behaviour.

It is doubtful if any other single emotion characterizes this period polit-ically in China more strongly than nationalism. The main reason for this is that the Chinese were reacting against their experience of the nineteenth and early twentieth century. A succession of wars and defeats inflicted on China by imperialist countries ranging from Britain to Japan culminated in the Boxer Rebellion. But there was more. The fact is that, when the twentieth century dawned, China was not actually ruled by the most populous people of China, called the Han, but by the Manchus who had conquered the country in the seventeenth century. So what the Han Chinese had to bear was a double domination: of foreign imperialism and a non-Han dynasty.

What are nationalism and imperialism? The notion of nationalism derives from that of 'the nation', a modern European concept. A nation refers to the group of peoples residing inside closely defined borders and owing loyalty to the state that rules the resulting territory. Nationalism is very much more than patriotism, which is simply love of country, because it is based on the supposition that the nation is the primary focus of political allegiance. So the people within the nation should give their loyalty not to the emperor or family, as had earlier been the case in China, but to the state that represents the nation. It follows that, by introducing the concept of nation, the European powers actually created the seeds of imperialism's decline in China, because nationalists like Sun Yat-sen, who arose in reaction to imperialism, did indeed strive for the people's loyalty to their own nation.

In contrast to the nation and nationalism, the ancient world knew about empires and their expansion beyond their borders. However, the modern forms of imperialism that concern this book actually derive from the Industrial Revolution in Europe in the late eighteenth century, being taken up later in Asia, notably by Japan. Imperialism involves the aggression of one country against another or others, and consequently has a bad reputation in the early twenty-first century. However, its results have been very broad, some of them being either necessary or good. The process of modernization in China resulted in large part from imperialism. Although the imperialists did not treat the Chinese as equals, yet there is irony in the fact that it was they who introduced such concepts as liberty, equality and democracy, which proved very attractive to some Chinese.

MODERNIZATION AND TRADITION

The reference to modernization brings us to another of the main dichotomies of China from 1900 to 1949: that between modernization and tradition. Virtually all Chinese leaders of the period have seen the quest for modernization as the way to save China. This path would enable China to catch up with the West, defeat imperialism and establish for China a respected position in the world community. One of the principal obstacles to achieving modernization is the force of tradition, or feudalism, the heavy weight of China's past.

Despite pejorative tags like feudalism, most Chinese are proud of the fact that China was once so mighty in the international community and produced so magnificent a culture, one that stands high among the world's civilizations. Feelings of nationalism might in some cases encourage people to see greatness in their own history and culture. But it became clear to all that, by the late eighteenth century, decline was setting in and the tenacity of some of the traditions was counted a major factor why China could make no further progress.

Scholars disagree on precisely when 'modern' China began, with dates ranging from as early as the Song dynasty (960–1279) to as late as 1976, when Mao Zedong died. Scholars of the People's Republic of China have generally considered the Opium (or First Sino-British) War of 1839–42 as the beginning of 'modern' China. Immanuel C. Y. Hsü's influential work *The Rise of Modern China* begins its account in the year 1600 but acknowledges the Opium War as one widely accepted boundary. Hsü (1995: 5–6) gives as his reason for the first date that this was the period when Chinese and Western history began to converge, and for the second that Western influence intensified in the nineteenth century (see also Cohen, 1984: 152–7).

The precise date when the processes of 'modernization' began in China depends on how modernity is conceived. There is a vast literature on 'modernization', which is well beyond the scope of the present book. Suffice it to observe that one important school of thought sees the 'modern' world as beginning, or lurching a giant step forward, with the Enlightenment and Industrial Revolution, taking place in Western Europe in the seventeenth and eighteenth centuries. By the late eighteenth century, when this process was gathering momentum in Europe, China was beginning its long decline. Modernity implies generally sustained and rapid economic growth, achieved through industry, advanced technology and communications, for example with trains and steamships replacing horse-drawn conveyances and sailing boats. Together with economic growth, a modern country can expect to find political forms that feature the decline or abolition of aristocracies, extensive participation of citizens in government and, frequently, the establishment of democratic institutions. A modernization process often sees a trend towards social equality, with greater social influence given to such groups as women and youth and more consideration accorded disadvantaged sectors.

FOREIGN IMPACT AND INTERNAL DYNAMIC

Immanuel Hsü's reasons for his views on when 'modern' China began are perfectly plausible. However, they have attracted criticism because of their implication that it was the West that created modern China, rather than any domestic impulses. Should not modernity in China depend on something China did itself, rather than something an outside force inflicted upon it? There is considerable irony in this dilemma, because the CCP, for all its patriotism or nationalism, has been strongest in pushing the view that the beginnings of 'modern' China coincided exactly with the first British imperialist attack on China, which launched the Opium War.

It remains true, as Fairbank notes **[Doc. 1, p. 118]**, that a striking feature of the Republican period from 1912 to 1949 is 'the degree of foreign influence upon and even participation in Chinese life during these years'. Nationalist Chinese resented the impact, and most bitterly that from Japan, that small eastern neighbour that had undertaken successful modernization and then turned to attack and invade what it should have respected as the parent civilization. But at the same time, Chinese governments and intellectuals began to see both the necessity and desirability of the modernization processes coming from outside its borders. It was modernity that allowed the West, and even Japan, to grow so great, while China languished in backwardness.

Yet it would be a mistake to see all 'modern' Chinese history in terms of foreign impact. Some scholars see Western influence as hardly extending outside the treaty ports, the Chinese economy being 'too gargantuan, too self-sufficient, and too poor to be substantially affected' by outside capital (Cohen, 1984: 125). Some aspects of Chinese development feature, in historical terms, a continuum over the whole period from the sixteenth century right down to the Japanese invasion of the 1930s and even beyond. Research into late imperial and Republican China in the last few decades has found an unexpected degree of internal dynamic. As one scholar has put it, such research poses a serious challenge to 'the old picture of a stagnant, slumbering, unchanging China, waiting to be delivered from its unfortunate condition of historylessness by a dynamic, restlessly changing, historyful West' (Cohen, 1984: 57).

2

Nineteenth-century Background

The nineteenth century was a period of rapid decline in China. It saw the ruling Manchu Qing dynasty weaken and the bureaucracy grow more corrupt, although with exceptions. China suffered from population explosion until about the middle of the century, leading to economic decline and famine. Rebellion erupted, the second half of the century witnessing outbreaks as serious as any in China's long history. Amid all these misfortunes, China had to cope with the beginnings and acceleration of Western and then Japanese imperialism, and although its responses were by no means ridiculous, they proved generally highly ineffective.

SOCIETY, ECONOMY AND POPULATION

The dominant ideology of traditional China was Confucianism, which was secular, hierarchical, authoritarian and family-centred. At the top was the imperial family, at that time drawn from a people called the Manchus. Just below was an amazingly small number (probably less than 10,000) of officials, called mandarins, who wielded very great power and enjoyed enormous social prestige. They were largely selected and maintained in office through a complex and stereotyped examination system. However, there was very serious discrimination against the majority ethnic group, the Han, and in favour of the Manchus right down to the end of the Qing dynasty. In the last decades of the dynasty, Manchus occupied about a quarter of official positions (Marsh, 1961: 48), even though they made up only some 1 per cent of the total population. In general, the higher the official, the more likely he was to be Manchu (see especially Rhoads, 2000: 45–8).

The overwhelming majority of the population was peasants, living in isolated villages. In line with Confucian hierarchical thinking, the family system gave a much higher status to males than to females and to old people than to young. If they could afford it, men were entitled to take concubines as well as a main wife. The most obvious sign of low female status was the ghastly and painful practice of foot-binding, which ordained that girls' feet be bound with tight cotton bandages from an early age to keep them small.

China's economy was dominated by agriculture. Although Confucian ideology was opposed to landlordism, it was nevertheless fairly widespread, varying in extent from place to place. Probably most families owned a portion of land, but also rented a patch from landlords, with many peasants owning no land at all but depending on what they could rent from a landlord. The most important industry was cotton. There was a good system of rivers and canals in some regions, facilitating domestic trade. In absolute terms, China's foreign trade was significant, especially with Southeast Asia, but was small compared to its domestic counterpart.

The population grew from about 143 million in 1741 to some 413 million in 1840, an average of 2.9 per cent annually. This is an extremely high growth rate, most of it occurring in the second part of the eighteenth century, not the early nineteenth. Although the amount of cultivated land grew by near 50 per cent over the same period, output failed to keep pace with population, dropping from 574 kilogrammes per person in 1741 to just over 300 in 1840 (see Mackerras and Yorke, 1991: 181). The situation worsened later in the nineteenth century, giving rise to serious famine. The worst single case occurred in northwestern China in 1876–9. A British diplomatic despatch to Foreign Secretary Lord Salisbury, dated 28 May 1878, claims that, over the winter of 1877–8, the single province of Shanxi lost some 5 million people, or about one-third of its population, due to famine (Mackerras, 1982: 137).

REBELLION

The Taiping Rebellion was by far the largest rebellion of Qing-dynasty China and among the largest in Chinese history. It wracked southern China from 1850 to 1866 and came near to overthrowing the dynasty. In the end it failed, but in the meantime had caused many millions of deaths.

The leader of the Taipings was Hong Xiuquan (1814–64), whose aspirations to join the bureaucracy had been thwarted by his failure in the official examinations. In March 1853 he and his supporters seized the Jiangsu provincial capital Nanjing, which they made the capital of their Heavenly Kingdom of Great Peace (*Taiping tianguo*), and soon after took Anqing, a major city in Anhui Province. In 1856 there was a major power struggle within the Taiping leadership, in which many people were killed.

The Taipings believed in an egalitarian ideology based on fundamentalist Christianity and various traditional Chinese ideas. Their system was a kind of theocracy, policy being determined largely according to religious criteria, and all money was channelled into a state treasury. In theory land was distributed equally according to family size, with men and women receiving equal shares, but in practice the rules were not properly applied. Despite claimed gender equality, in practice the leaders had large harems, the size determined according to rank, while at the same time they forced their followers to practice segregation of the sexes.

The Western powers were at first very sympathetic to the Taipings, due to a shared belief in Christianity. However, early in 1862 they changed their policy decisively, because the Taipings threatened Shanghai, the main treaty port, and soon after they even sent troops against the Taipings. Although their participation in the war was important, it was not decisive. The Qing dynasty's Hunan Army had already inflicted major defeats on the Taipings, including the recapture of Anqing in September 1861 after a long siege. Nanjing fell to the Hunan Army in July 1864, and some 100,000 Taipings either committed suicide or were slaughtered by its troops.

Among numerous other nineteenth-century rebellions, one of particular significance for its territorial implications was that of Yakub Beg, which affected the Muslim areas of China's far west from the mid-1860s until 1878. In 1867 Yakub Beg declared himself the ruler of an independent state of Kashgaria, which lay in territory the court regarded as Chinese. In the debate over whether or not it was worth the money, effort and blood to suppress the rebellion, the main proponent of intervention was Zuo Zongtang (1812–85), who was actively suppressing Muslim rebellion in Gansu and Shaanxi Provinces from the late 1860s. The court gave its final approval for a war against Yakub Beg in early 1876, in particular giving Zuo Zongtang permission to raise a large foreign loan. He succeeded in suppressing Yakub Beg's independent kingdom the next year, with Yakub Beg himself committing suicide in May. In November 1884 the region was established as a province of China with the name Xinjiang, meaning 'new frontier'. If Zuo Zongtang had failed, it is doubtful that Xinjiang would still be part of China.

THE WESTERN IMPACT AND THE UNEQUAL TREATIES

Although the Qing dynasty's victories against these rebellions show that it was far from being prepared simply to give up, the wars certainly went some way towards exhausting the court, both psychologically and financially.

Meanwhile, the dynasty faced serious problems from British and other Western incursions along the eastern coast. Qing troops were involved in various wars against the Western powers, virtually all of them ending with major concessions forced through treaty upon unhappy China. In this section a few of the issues involved in the treaties are taken up.

The first of the 'unequal treaties' was the Treaty of Nanjing, signed on 29 August 1842, which ended the Opium War. The treaty opened several ports to foreign trade, including Guangzhou (Canton) and Shanghai, the first of the 'treaty ports', and ceded the small island of Hong Kong to Britain. One of the clauses of the Treaty of Nanjing stipulated that China indemnify Britain. What this actually meant was that China should pay for the war that had been launched against it. Seen from China's point of view, this was particularly humiliating, since it had not wanted the war in the first place. Worse still, it became a precedent that was followed by others as they waged war against an increasingly helpless China. Another major precedent was set by a supplement to this treaty, the so-called 'most-favoured-nation' clause. This meant that the signatory of the treaty would automatically receive any rights the Chinese might, in the future, concede to any other nation, a totally open-ended concession that was to prove extremely expensive for China.

In 1844 China signed the Treaty of Wangxia with the USA and the Treaty of Whampoa with France. These two treaties included articles of great importance.

The first was the granting of extraterritoriality. This concept meant that foreigners in China were subject not to Chinese law but to that of their own country. In the nineteenth century the Western powers assumed that all persons were subject to the laws of the country where they were residing, no matter what their citizenship, and that is still the situation under international law. Little did the Chinese realise what they were giving up when they agreed to extraterritoriality. In the course of time, foreign powers set up their own courts in China, which differed greatly from the Chinese courts in the laws they followed, in the criteria they applied, and in the judgements they reached. It was frequently even possible for foreigners in China to get away with crimes for which they would have been severely punished in their own country.

Notwithstanding this agreement, in 1856 a Chinese court actually had a French missionary decapitated, as part of a general policy of persecution of Christians in one part of south China. The action provoked a war between China on the one hand and Britain and France on the other. The result was the occupation of the Chinese capital Beijing by British and French troops in October 1860 and the near total destruction, over several days that month, of the vast and magnificent Old Summer Palace west of the city.

China signed four further agreements: two Treaties of Tianjin and two Conventions of Beijing, one of each with Britain and France. Two issues are worth comment here. One is that China allowed foreign residents in Beijing. The Chinese tradition was that a foreign embassy came to China for a specific purpose, carried out its task and then left. China had fought against the idea of allowing the representatives of foreign powers actually to reside semi-permanently in its capital city. The other matter was to allow total freedom of movement for Christian missionaries in China. The implication that Westerners could propagate their own religion anywhere in China was to bring important results in the coming decades.

THE SINO-JAPANESE WAR ENDS THE TRIBUTE SYSTEM

For many centuries China had operated its foreign relations under a system that Western scholars have dubbed 'the tribute system' or 'the Chinese world order'. The essence of the system was that surrounding countries sent in tribute to the Chinese emperor and paid him homage as the ruler of the region's most powerful country. Those envoys fortunate enough to be received by the Chinese monarch had to undergo a very special and elaborate ritual, which included the famous *ketou*, usually romanized kowtow (literally 'knock the head'). The envoy knelt down and knocked his head against the ground to symbolize his reverence for the emperor's authority and person. The Confucian ideology on which this 'world order' was based required that the emperor, or *tianzi* ('son of heaven'), should enshrine virtue, thus deserving the homage paid him, and treat all foreign potentates with absolute impartiality. There was certainly no concept of the equality of nations in this system. On the other hand, only in the most extreme of circumstances would the Chinese intervene militarily in the territories of the 'tribute' countries.

The advent of Western imperialism had chipped away at this system, but not destroyed it. Among all the tribute countries, the most important was Korea. Although very isolated, even known as the 'hermit kingdom', Korea continued to send tribute to China and was heavily influenced by the Chinese Confucian political system and culture. While the Chinese did not generally interfere in its internal affairs, they regarded Korea as part of their tribute system and a 'dependency' (*fanshu*) [Doc. 2, p. 119].

Following the Meiji Restoration of 1868, Japan began a successful modernization process and not long afterwards began to evince signs of imperialist pretensions in China and elsewhere. In the mid-1870s Japan began to compete with China for influence in Korea which, under pressure, signed with Japan the 1876 Treaty of Kanghwa. A fiercely anti-foreign rebellion called the Tonghak (literally 'Eastern Learning'), a little similar to the Taipings in China, had begun in the 1860s in Korea, but in the 1890s erupted into major violence, even threatening the capital Seoul in May 1894. Korean King Kojong requested military assistance from China to put down the rebellion. When the Chinese agreed, Japan soon decided to send troops to Korea, taking over the imperial palace and in July installing a government suited to their interests **[Doc. 2, p. 119]**.

On 1 August 1894 China and Japan declared war against each other. The war was fought first in Korea itself, followed by a major naval battle, China being totally defeated in both cases. Japanese troops then invaded China, seizing territory and routing their Chinese counterparts. Li Hongzhang (1823–1901), the effective Chinese foreign minister in the absence of such a post in the Chinese bureaucracy, went to Japan, signing the Treaty of Shimonoseki in April 1895. The provisions included handing Taiwan over to the Japanese and paying an enormous indemnity.

There were two major implications of this treaty. First, this was the first time that China had been defeated not by a Western power but by an Asian neighbour. This was an enormous humiliation for China and it showed the degree to which Japan had followed the Western lead in imperialist behaviour and in modernizing itself, especially its military forces. Second, the war went a long way towards handing Korea over to the Japanese. Not only was this the last nail in the coffin of the Chinese tribute system but it also opened the way for Japan to take Korea over as a formal colony, which it did in 1910.

In the last years of the century, following China's defeat by Japan, the foreign powers stepped up their pressures on China. The year 1898 saw the 'scramble for concessions', with Britain, Germany, France and Russia taking out leases and other rights over Chinese territory. Among these, by far the most important, and best known, was the ninety-nine-year lease which Britain took over the 'New Territories' of Hong Kong. The agreement, which the Chinese court approved early in June 1898, provided that these territories would revert to China on 1 July 1997.

THE BEGINNINGS OF REFORM AND MODERNIZATION

The reaction of the Chinese against these various imperialist onslaughts was one of great confusion. At court, one faction wished to cling to the old ways, regarding anything foreign as useless and inapplicable to Chinese conditions.

But gradually it became obvious that only by adopting certain aspects of Western technology could China hope to cope with the West. In July 1862 a College of Foreign Languages began taking students, expanding its curriculum to mathematics and astronomy in 1866. Arsenals were established. In 1868 the Fuzhou Dockyard begin formal operations, and the same year the Jiangnan Arsenal completed work on its first steamship, called *Tianji*.

These preliminary successes did not stop opposition from conservatives. In response to the decision by the College of Foreign Languages to expand its curriculum, the Manchu official Woren (d. 1871) wrote a memorial to the Emperor in 1867 arguing that astronomy and mathematics were of very little use, and that the teaching of such subjects by Westerners in the College of Foreign Languages would cause great harm. Woren believed that only an emphasis on Confucian values like propriety and righteousness could benefit the nation. And there were others like Woren who did all they could to impede anything that seemed Western.

Yet many could see the need for modernization of the sort that the West had used to empower itself to China's detriment. At the forefront of the modernization effort at this stage was Li Hongzhang, who became the patron of many technical innovations and enterprises using modern machinery. He was a strong advocate of the building of steamships and, later, railways. In 1872 he supported a proposal for a steamship line. He also sponsored the first permanent telegraph lines in China.

China's defeat by Japan in 1895 gave further impetus to the need for reform and modernization. In the wake of that disaster the modernizer and moderate reformer Zhang Zhidong (1837–1909), known especially for his activism in railway building and for setting up China's first major coal, iron, and steel complex in eastern Hubei, pushed his notion of 'essence and usefulness' (Chinese *ti yong*). The meaning of the phrase was that the way to develop China was to leave Chinese learning as the foundation, but use Western learning for practical purposes.

In 1898 a group of reformers, led by Kang Youwei (1858–1927) and Liang Qichao, convinced the **Guangxu Emperor** (r. 1875–1908) of the need for reform. On 11 June he issued an edict that began the **Hundred Days' Reform**. He ordered that the education system be changed to reflect modern realities. The examination system should be restructured to eliminate the old-fashioned format of essay writing, schools should offer both Chinese and Western learning, and special institutes should be founded for the study of such modern ventures as mining, industry and railways. The edict also gave attention to the armed forces, ordering the building of a fleet of warships and the standardization of army drill along Western lines. The Emperor also gave several of the reform faction, notably Kang Youwei, senior positions at court.

Guangxu Emperor (1871–1908): Ruled as Chinese emperor from 1875 to his death. He was the nephew of the Empress Dowager Cixi, who in 1898 had him put under house arrest to counter the changes he had introduced through the Hundred Days' Reform, although, most of the changes came into effect following the Boxer Rebellion of 1900.

Hundred Days' Reform: The name given to the reform period from 11 June to 21 September 1898, when the Qing Emperor promoted policies of reform.

The **Empress Dowager Cixi**, Guangxu's aunt, who had seized effective power in the early 1860s, was alarmed at the extent of the reforms suggested. They seemed to her to threaten the ruling dynasty and she was afraid of the British and French influences that appeared to operate on the reform faction. On 21 September, 102 days after Guangxu's edict, she carried out her own *coup d'etat*, had the Guangxu Emperor placed under house arrest and countered his reform measures. Kang Youwei and Liang Qichao fled abroad. This first major imperially sponsored attempt at extensive reform had failed.

Empress Dowager Cixi (1835–1908): Aunt of the Guangxu Emperor, and the effective ruler of China from the early 1860s until her death. Strongly opposed the Reform Movement of 1898, but still presided over some important changes in Chinese politics and society after the Boxer Rebellion of 1900.

Part 2

CHINA IN TRANSFORMATION: CHRONOLOGICAL TREATMENT

3

The End of the Qing period, 1900–11

Beginning with the Boxer Rebellion and ending with the fall of the Qing dynasty, the years 1900 to 1911 formed a highly dramatic period in Chinese history. The Boxer Rebellion and the eight-power invasion it provoked saw China at its most supine. But it would be a mistake to imagine that the Qing dynasty simply did nothing but allowed itself to collapse without a fight. In fact, the first decade of the century saw some very important reforms and innovations of a scope large enough to change the face of China. And it was the period when nationalism first became a truly vital force in Chinese history [**Doc. 3, p. 119**].

THE BOXER REBELLION AND REACTION

In the last years of the nineteenth century, a rebel group fired by intense resentment of foreign missionaries and power began to make itself felt in northwest Shandong Province, south of Beijing. They called themselves 'the Righteous and Harmonious Fists' (*Yihe quan*) because they practised a kind of boxing for which they claimed magic power. This is the origin of the name Boxers, by which they have become known.

In November 1897 two German Catholic missionaries were killed in Juye, in the far west of Shandong. The Germans reacted by occupying the port city of Qingdao early the next month. Meanwhile, the last years of the nineteenth century saw a combination of flood and drought in Shandong. In the summer of 1898 serious flooding affected over a million people in Shandong, leading to harvest failure.

The effect was dramatic. The Boxers blamed the foreigners for the disasters afflicting China. They raised the slogan 'Revive the Qing, destroy the foreigners'. Although almost completely lacking in leadership, they succeeded

in gaining widespread support from peasants, itinerants, artisans, canal boat-
men and others from the poor sectors of society. The great majority were
men, but there were also female Boxer groups, the most important of them
consisting of young girls and women, aged about twelve to eighteen, 'whose
female powers were invoked to fight the "pollution" of the Chinese Christian
women, which was believed to erode the strength of Boxer men' (Spence,
1990: 232–3).

The Boxers moved northwards and by the early summer of 1900 groups
of Boxers had entered the capital Beijing and the nearby major city of Tianjin.
They harassed, and even killed, Chinese Christians or those who had been
influenced by foreigners, as well as some foreigners. They were also hostile
to the kind of modernization they associated with foreigners, for instance
cutting telegraph lines.

The powers, on their part, were totally alarmed by the rise of this extraordinary force with its ragged, low-society and apparently irrational and
murderous followers. Early in April 1900 the main Western powers had
already demanded that the Qing should eliminate the Boxers, threatening
to call in foreign troops to carry out the task unless the Qing had done so
within two months. Shortly afterwards, the world's eight major powers,
Britain, Germany, France, Russia, the USA, Japan, Italy and Austria-Hungary,
sent a large force, which on 17 June captured the Dagu Forts outside Tianjin,
opening the way to an invasion of China. This was the first and only time in
history that these eight powers all stood on the same side in battle.

The Chinese government did not know how to react. Many within it were
sympathetic to the Boxers, or even actively supportive, because they were
prepared to stand up to the foreigners and, after all, called for Qing revival.
On 19 June the court demanded the withdrawal of all foreign legations, the
next day the Boxers began their 'siege of the legations', and on 21 June the
court actually issued an edict declaring war on the powers.

Although the Boxers and some Qing troops put up sharp resistance
against the foreign forces, in fact they were very disorganized and the main
modernized Qing troops stood aside, refusing to take part. On 14 July the
allied troops of the eight powers seized Tianjin and soon after marched
towards Beijing. They entered the capital on 14 August, lifting the siege and
beginning savage and extended plunder. The next day the Empress Dowager
fled from Beijing towards Xi'an, taking the Emperor with her, her flight prov-
ing expensive and burdensome to the people along the way, and provoking
resentment and contempt towards her as a selfish coward [Doc. 4, p. 120].

On 7 September 1901 China signed a humiliating protocol with the
powers. Several of those officials who had sided most ardently with the
Boxers were punished by being forced to commit suicide, executed, exiled
or posthumously degraded. In addition, China was forced to pay a gigantic

indemnity to pay for the war and subsequent occupation, to raze the Dagu Forts and allow foreign occupation of many cities in north China. So disastrous was the outcome of the Boxer Rebellion for China that some people believed that China might be partitioned and colonized **[Doc. 5, p. 121]**.

POST-BOXER NATIONALISM AND REFORM

However, such was not to be. The late Mary Wright, a major historian of the period, has written: 'Rarely in history has a single year marked as dramatic a watershed as did 1900 in China' **[Doc. 3, p. 119]**. She argues that everybody in China drew the lesson from the Boxer disaster that China *must* reform or it would go under, with the Qing dynasty facing the ultimate disaster of overthrow and national disintegration.

So one of the results of the Boxer Rebellion was a rise in nationalism. This was not absolutely new to the period, and was one of the forces leading to the Boxer Rebellion itself. Yet there is no doubt that nationalism took on a new impetus from the beginning of the twentieth century. Since it was the major powers that had inflicted the humiliation upon China, the focus of nationalism was the desire to roll back the forces and influences of imperialism in China.

Given the dreadful instability to afflict China in this decade, discussed in the next section, it is important not to exaggerate the power of the court to establish its own control throughout the territories it claimed as China. Yet the fact is that the first decade of the twentieth century did see the Chinese government consolidate its rule in several major frontier regions, and its degree of success was quite impressive. One area affected was Tibet, where the British, against vehement Chinese opposition, were making inroads in 1903–4, when Colonel Francis Younghusband led his expedition to Lhasa. In 1906 the court sent Zhang Yintang to take control of Tibetan affairs, and he proved very much more assertive in governing the region and stamping out corruption there than his predecessor had been. Early in 1910 the Qing court actually sent troops to Lhasa, the Chinese government making a formal statement in terms of China's sovereign rights in the region in April.

Even before the Boxer Protocol was signed, the court issued a decree announcing its intentions to undertake reform and asking for advice on how to implement it. Very soon, attempts began towards reform in a range of areas. These included raising the status of women and youth, and instituting some far-reaching and much needed changes in the educational system, to be discussed in Chapters 11 and 12. One item of social reform was a campaign to suppress opium. On 20 September 1906 the court issued an edict banning opium altogether, with plans to eliminate all its evil effects within a decade. According to Mary Wright, the results of the campaign were 'astonishing'. She adds: 'The anti-opium campaign may have been the largest and most vigorous effort in world history to stamp out an established social evil'. By the time of the revolution, food crops had replaced the poppy in some four-fifths of the land where it had once prevailed, and 'whatever opium smoking continued was done in private' (Wright, 1968: 14).

In April 1901 the court ordered the establishment of a Bureau of Government Affairs to formulate a reform programme. The processes leading to modern government began. The crucial factor of constitutionalism is the subject of a later section, but it is noteworthy that even in 1901 a modern Ministry of Foreign Affairs was established, with similar bodies following later. Among these the Bureau of Customs, set up in May 1906, was particularly important, because it took some of the control of Chinese customs away from the foreign powers. Sir Robert Hart had been Inspector General of the Chinese Customs since 1865. He was no doubt genuinely dedicated to the service of China, but what matters here is that by 1906 the trend of the times made it impossible for a foreigner to be so exclusively dominant in a position of such importance for China's political economy.

The last decade of the Qing appears to have seen the beginnings of the development of a commercial bourgeoisie in China. An edict of 1903 specifically encouraged industry and commerce, thus reversing the discrimination that merchants suffered under Confucian ideology. Marie-Claire Bergère believes that the nascent commercial bourgeoisie merged with the old gentry, who had been in decline since the late decades of the nineteenth century and suffered greatly from the abolition of the traditional examination system in 1905, forming a class she calls the 'merchant-gentry'. This class was 'composed of the influential people of each locality, closely connected with land ownership, but not above taking the opportunity to derive profit from investment in modern business ventures' (Wright, 1968: 240). There may well have been an increasing identity or self-awareness among the bourgeoisie, one expression of this being that many chambers of commerce came into being from 1904 onwards. This bourgeoisie was definitely nationalist in feeling, resisting foreign privileges and demanding strong central government both able and willing to provide conditions for a national market to develop and enforcing a modern commercial code.

In the first decade of the twentieth century railway building expanded greatly. At the end of 1896 there were only 600 kilometres of railways in China, but, though the Boxers were anti-modernist and went as far as actually tearing up tracks, the disastrous episode showed the advantages of being able to move troops quickly by railway. According to one authority, the Boxers may have ended in defeat for China, but 'railways emerged with greater prestige' (Spence, 1990: 250). Between 1900 and 1905 no less than 5,200 kilometres of railways were built in China. April 1910 saw the completion of the Yunnan–Vietnam railway and in October 1911 that from Guangzhou to Kowloon started taking traffic.

The railways also became bound up with the issue of nationalism. This was because almost all funds for building railways were foreign. In the middle of the decade the recovery of railway rights became a very popular issue, with numerous demonstrations and the establishment of 'railway rights-recovery' groups. Unfortunately, attempts to obtain local capital from those both willing and able to invest in the railways proved only partly successful, so in May 1911 the Qing court issued a decree nationalizing the main railways and indemnifying private owners. We shall see in the next chapter that this policy was to lead directly to the 1911 Revolution, making the railways closely involved in the politics of the last days of the Qing dynasty.

THE RUSSO-JAPANESE WAR

While the 1900 Boxer crisis was in progress in Beijing, Russian troops marched into Manchuria, arguing that they were suppressing 'rioters'. They met very little resistance, and, by the end of September 1900, had occupied virtually the whole territory. However, although it was very humiliating, this disaster did bring about two positive results. First, it added to the sense of nationalism and the desire for China to assert itself among the powers. Second, several of the powers were not at all happy at the advantages the Russians were demanding for themselves on the near-corpse of the giant China. In particular, Japan had its own interests in Manchuria and it was not willing to yield them. Britain took a similar stand and even concluded an agreement with Japan early in 1902, by which each country would help the other to protect interests in China or Korea. Although negotiations took place between Russia and Japan to try and reach some *modus vivendi*, neither side was prepared to give up vital interests in Manchuria or Korea; and the result was war.

In the event it was Japan that started the war on 8 February 1904 by attacking Russia's naval squadron at Lüshun (also called Port Arthur at that time). To Japan's extreme annoyance, China chose to be neutral in the Russo-Japanese war **[Doc. 6, p. 121]**. This was a particularly savage war with very heavy casualties. The biggest battle was that for Shenyang, in February and March 1905. Japanese troops numbered 250,000 and Russian 300,000, some 90,000 Russian casualties and 70,000 Japanese resulting. The Japanese won both this battle and the war very convincingly. The Treaty of

Portsmouth, New Hampshire, which ended the war, was signed in September 1905, with most previously Russian interests in Manchuria ceded to Japan, which also tightened its grip on Korea.

Two points about this war are of the utmost significance. First, although China was not involved in the war, most of the fighting actually took place on Chinese soil, in particular the enormous Battle of Shenyang. The second point is that this was the first war in modern history between a European and an Asian power which the Asian had actually won, and decisively. The lesson was very clear for China: it should follow the Japanese road to development by adopting modern practices originally found in the West.

CONSTITUTIONAL REFORM

From a political point of view one of the most significant reforms of the Qing's last decade was the beginnings of constitutionalism. Liang Qichao was the most prominent of those who, having abandoned radicalism, turned to constitutional monarchy as a favoured alternative to revolution, and he became the leading theorist of the constitutionalists. One of the main lessons of Japan's victory over Russia in the war of 1904–5 was that China should adopt Japan's path of constitutionalism. Zhang Jian (1853–1926), the noted scholar and industrialist who later became the chairman of the Jiangsu Provincial Assembly, proclaimed that 'the victory of Japan and the defeat of Russia are the victory of constitutionalism and the defeat of monarchism' (Hsü, 1995: 412). In December 1905 the court sent a mission to various countries, including Britain, France and Japan, to examine foreign forms of government. It reported that Japan's was the model with the most to offer China.

On 1 September 1906 the court announced that it would have a constitution drafted, although it laid down no timeframe for doing so. There is little doubt that the Empress Dowager allowed this step rather reluctantly, because she disliked constitutionalism and resented such obstacles to court power. On the other hand, if she disliked constitutionalism, then she hated the idea of revolution much more. And that loomed as the most likely alternative.

In August 1908 the court accepted a draft constitution for a constitutional monarchy. This declared that the Qing would rule for ever and defined the powers of the emperor, the duties of ministers, the rights and obligations of citizens, and the rights, as well as limitations, of parliament. Nine years of constitutional reform should follow, at the end of which the court would promulgate a constitution and convene a national parliament.

Meanwhile, the court had accepted the need for elections for assemblies at provincial level and local councils. And from February to June 1909 elections took place in all the provinces, the resultant assemblies actually meeting in mid-October the same year. Despite great reluctance from the court, representatives of these provincial assemblies successfully petitioned for a national assembly, which the court stipulated would consist of 200 members, half elected by the provincial assemblies and half selected from among the imperial family, aristocrats, officials and scholars. The National Assembly met for the first time on 3 October 1910. The Guangxu Emperor had died in November 1908, the day before the Empress Dowager, and the successor Emperor Puyi (1906–67) was only four years old. So it was the Regent Zaifeng who opened the Assembly.

The voters at the 1909 elections were drawn from particular groups of society, such as gentry, metropolitan degree holders (*jinshi*) and other scholars. The proportion of electoral voters to population varied from province to province. It was highest in Zhili Province, the area around the capital Beijing, where there were 162,585 voters in a population of nearly 26 million, or 0.625 per cent (Wright, 1968: 150). In other words elections did not mean anything even remotely resembling one person, one vote.

Yet, for all their shortcomings, the fact is these were the first elections in Chinese history. Moreover, the members were anything but government stooges. They protested loudly and at length when dissatisfied, and one of the actions of the new National Assembly was to present a petition, claiming 25 million signatures, for the immediate convening of a genuine parliament. Such a 'mass movement', based on constitutionalism rather than rebellion, was totally unprecedented in Chinese history. The Assembly members attacked the Qing regime for corruption, and some of them finally opted to join the revolution.

4

The Revolution of Sun Yat-sen

This chapter focuses on the 1911 Revolution and the career of its main leader Sun Yat-sen (1866–1925) down to the end of 1913. Sun is one of the very few twentieth-century Chinese leaders to enjoy a good reputation among virtually all Chinese, including both the Communist and Nationalist Parties. Often called 'the father of the nation' (*guofu*), it was Sun Yat-sen whose revolution succeeded in overthrowing the monarchy in China and developing the ideology of the Nationalist Party. Notwithstanding these successes, Sun Yat-sen did not enjoy state power for long. One of his Western biographers, noting that 'persistence rather than brilliance distinguished his performance', regards his high reputation as due more to his role as 'the symbol of China's quest for resurgence' than to his achievements (Schiffrin, 1980: 4, 3; see also Schiffrin, 1968; Martin, 1944; Wilbur, 1976).

SUN YAT-SEN'S EARLY CAREER AND REVOLUTIONARY ACTIVITIES

Born to a peasant family in a village near Guangzhou, Sun Yat-sen lived for four years in Hawai'i in his youth and trained as a doctor in Hong Kong. Both places exercised considerable influence over him, especially their Westernized institutions, approaches to knowledge and economic development. In 1894 he wrote to Li Hongzhang in Tianjin, the effective Chinese foreign minister, with the aim of trying to secure employment. The message he proposed was that China should copy the West's path to prosperity and power, which lay in the effective development of human potential through universal education and the full exploitation of the world's resources. As the reader will recall from Chapter 2, Li had other things on his mind, especially Korea, over which the Sino-Japanese War was shortly to break out. He probably did not even read Sun's letter, and certainly did not see the young man. Sun's disappointment convinced him that he should try to overthrow the establishment that had ignored him.

In November 1894 Sun Yat-sen set up his first anti-Manchu association, the Society for the Revival of China (*Xing Zhong hui*), in Hawai'i, where he hoped to raise money. He soon returned to Hong Kong and Guangzhou and developed a plot for late October 1895 to seize Guangzhou, making it his revolutionary headquarters. However, the plot was discovered and the Society defeated, with many of its members captured and some killed. The 'first revolution', as historians know this event, had failed.

Sun went abroad to the USA and England for propaganda and other purposes. In the USA he made no headway in gaining support from overseas Chinese, but did alarm the Chinese government, with the result that the Chinese minister in Washington alerted his counterpart in London of Sun's travels. When Sun arrived in London in October 1896 he was kidnapped and detained at the Chinese legation, but released, after an imprisonment of twelve days, through the agency of his friend Dr James Cantlie, whom he had known when training as a doctor in Hong Kong. The kidnap and imprisonment turned out to be a blessing in disguise, because the British and world press gave it coverage, so that it had the effect of making Sun suddenly famous. In England, where he stayed nine months, Sun first became aware that even in the industrialized West there was still a social problem and people were not necessarily rich or contented. He reached the conclusion that a social revolution was inevitable in the advanced West but persisted in thinking, as Martin Bernal has remarked, that in backward China 'it was still possible to prevent the injustice of the class system and the catastrophe of a violent social revolution' (Wright, 1968: 103).

After departing from England, Sun spent some time in Japan, hoping to win support there, since the Chinese population was much larger than in Europe. However, Japan proved a disappointment, since the Chinese population was largely apolitical or conservative, and he attracted no more than a hundred or so supporters. Worse still, Kang Youwei, who had fled to Japan following the failure of the Hundred Days' Reform, was very hostile towards him. He and Liang Qichao had established the Protect the Emperor Society (*Baohuang dang*), which was reformist but monarchist, and hence against the notion of revolution. Kang despised Sun as a 'rebel without dignity, won over by Western materialistic ideas' (Bergère, 1998: 77), while the different world-views of the two men 'were exacerbated by a mutual jealousy' as well as by different social origins and intellectual backgrounds (Bergère, 1998: 78).

THE UNITED LEAGUE AND REVOLUTION OF 1911

Chinese United League: *Tongmeng hui*, the revolutionary group set up by Sun Yat-sen in 1905 in Tokyo.

Yet after much more travel Sun returned to Tokyo and it was there that he established the **Chinese United League** (*Tongmeng hui*) on 20 August 1905. There were about seventy members at the inaugural meeting, with significantly more soon afterwards. Among the founders Sun himself became president, with Huang Xing (d. 1916) and Song Jiaoren (1882–1913) among the leading cadre.

The League's manifesto comprised four basic points **[Doc. 8, p. 123]**:

- expulsion of the Manchus;
- restoration of Chinese rule;
- establishment of a republic;
- equalization of land rights.

Nationalism (in Sun's three principles): *Minzu zhuyi.*

Democracy (in Sun's three principles): *Minquan zhuyi.*

People's livelihood (in Sun's three principles): *Minsheng zhuyi.*

These ideas were the basis of Sun's three principles of the people: **nationalism, democracy** and **people's livelihood**, discussed in Chapter 6 **[Docs 15, 16 and 17, pp. 128–30]**.

At this stage two features are striking in the United League's ideology. The first is that two of the three principles implied nationalism, but it was a nationalism aimed more against the Manchus than against the foreign powers. The first, and presumably most important, of the points actually refers to expelling the Manchus from China and disposing of those who resisted. Feelings against the Manchu government and even people continued to be very strong, especially among the revolutionaries (Rhoads, 2000: 12–18). The influential young pamphleteer Zou Rong put out a nationalist tract in 2003 that speaks of the Manchus in extremely hostile, even racist, terms **[Doc. 9, p. 124]**. The second feature is the radical socialist nature of the last point, on equal land rights.

The pace of revolutionary activity quickened. The 'first revolution' of 1895 had been followed by another failed one in 1900. But between 1906 and 1911 there were eight, making ten in all. All took place in the south, especially in Guangdong. The last occurred in April 1911, when Huang Xing led an attempt to seize the Guangdong provincial capital, Guangzhou. Although it was defeated, with many student revolutionaries returned from Japan among those killed, this Guangzhou uprising was a great shock to the Qing court and, with the benefit of hindsight, appears to have presaged the successful attempt at the Hubei capital Wuchang later the same year.

In July 1911 Song Jiaoren and others devised a plan from Shanghai to strike at the central provinces of China in an eleventh attempt to bring down the Qing dynasty. In Hubei there were already organizations affiliated with the United League. One of special importance included members of the Qing dynasty's recently established New Army who had gone over to the revolutionary cause.

In attempting to nationalize the railways in May 1911, as discussed in Chapter 3, the Qing dynasty's policy was to indemnify all those who had invested private money. But because the various provinces had received uneven treatment in the indemnification process, serious resentments flared up against the policy. Sichuan had fared the worst, as a result of which its provincial assembly not only protested very strongly to the central government but also organized a mass movement of students and others. On 7 September 1911 the newly appointed governor of Sichuan, Zhao Erfeng (d. 1911), anxious to please the central government, actually sent troops against demonstrators, demanding the cancellation of railway nationalization in their province, and over thirty were killed. Although the members of the provincial assembly were constitutional monarchists, the failure of the Manchu government to heed their protests made many sympathetic to the revolution.

The Qing government sent troops to Sichuan from Hubei to suppress the disorder, leaving the way open for the revolutionaries to take advantage of a military vacuum in Hubei. On 9 October 1911 some revolutionaries in the Russian Concession of Hankou, which with Wuchang and Hanyang actually forms a triple city known as Wuhan, accidentally let off a bomb from among those they intended to use against the Qing. The Qing police reacted by arresting many revolutionaries. Two battalions of the New Army that had gone over to the revolution decided to seize the government munition depot in Wuchang and were able to take control of the city on 10 October.

This Wuchang uprising, which in Taiwan is still celebrated as National Day, was the spark that set the whole of China on fire. In a chain reaction the various provinces declared themselves independent of the dynasty. By the end of 1911 more or less the whole country had declared itself in support of the revolution.

When the Wuchang uprising occurred, Sun Yat-sen was in Colorado. Rather than return home immediately, he decided to seek international support for the revolution, which he knew would be crucial to its success. He did not actually get back to China until 25 December. The revolutionaries had already decided on Nanjing, capital of Jiangsu Province near Shanghai, as the capital of the provisional Republican government. They were much stronger in the south than the north, where the Qing court was located. On 1 January 1912 the Republic of China (ROC) was formally proclaimed in Nanjing, with Sun Yat-sen as provisional president.

YUAN SHIKAI BETRAYS THE REVOLUTION

What was unfortunate about the Revolution of 1911 was that no sooner had it triumphed than it stared defeat and betrayal in the face. This was largely because of a former stalwart of the Qing government, Yuan Shikai (1859–1916), who was prepared to cross over to the revolution, but at the same time manipulate it to his personal advantage. The trouble was that Yuan controlled the army in the north and, at the end of 1911, most revolutionaries believed him to be the only person who could prevent the outbreak of civil war and persuade the Qing Emperor to abdicate. Yuan exacted a high price for his support of the revolution, namely that he would replace Sun Yat-sen as president (Young, 1977).

On 12 February 1912, the last Qing Emperor Puyi abdicated and at the same time appointed Yuan Shikai as plenipotentiary to form a Republican government. Yuan issued a statement pledging absolute loyalty to the Republic, adding that he would never allow the system of monarchy to reappear in China. The idealistic Sun Yat-sen bowed out in his favour, probably realising that the military realities gave him no choice. The Senate appointed Yuan as provisional ROC president on 15 February. The next month it adopted a revised provisional constitution for the ROC, under which elections took place at the end of the year. Song Jiaoren, who was a very skilful political operator, organized the Nationalist Party (*Guomin dang*) to compete in the elections, and succeeded in bringing it a very handsome victory.

However, Yuan Shikai had no intention of allowing constitutional processes to run their course. He immediately began taking all measures at his disposal to seize full power. He moved the capital back to Beijing, where his main power base lay. He put all his own henchmen in the powerful executive positions and marginalized the revolutionaries. He tried to bribe Song Jiaoren to his side, but on 22 March 1913 the Nationalist Party leader died through an assassin's bullet. Legal processes failed to implicate Yuan Shikai, but since these were themselves full of intrigue and murder, most people believed – and still believe – that the president was the one mainly responsible for Song Jiaoren's death. To strengthen his position against the Nationalists, Yuan Shikai also negotiated an enormous 'reorganization loan' with the foreign powers. When Sun Yat-sen and Huang Xing urged the Parliament to reject the loan, Yuan had the building surrounded with troops, forcing the measure through.

Feeling betrayed by these developments, the Nationalists attempted a 'Second Revolution' in mid-1913 to regain their influence. Yuan sent out troops, easily defeating them. In October 1913 he simply declared the Nationalist Party seditious and ordered its dissolution, hunting its remaining representatives from Parliament. The next month, Sun Yat-sen departed for

Japan, 'driven once more into exile from his own country, his republican dreams in ruins' (Spence, 1990: 281). Early the following year Yuan Shikai followed up his dissolution of the Nationalist Party with that of the National Assembly itself.

Despite his early-1912 protestations of eternal loyalty to republicanism, Yuan Shikai did in fact try to set himself up as emperor. He took several moves to forestall possible foreign opposition to his action, the most important of them being substantive agreement to Twenty-one Demands that Japan made on China in January 1915, having the overall effect of vastly increasing Japanese interests, influence and even control in China. Late in 1915 Yuan declared his intention to become emperor at the beginning of the following year. A storm of protest erupted in the provinces, with declarations of independence following, and Yuan was forced to give up the plan. He died in June 1916 of uremia, and perhaps fury and frustration, a disappointed man reviled by virtually all his countrymen for his corruption, deceit, double-dealing and megalomania.

REASONS FOR THE SUCCESS OF THE 1911 REVOLUTION

Why did the 1911 Revolution succeed in overthrowing the Qing monarchy?

The nationalism spawned by China's humiliations and by the Boxer Rebellion was certainly a major factor. It was directed against the Manchus because they were not Chinese, as shown by the fact that the United League placed 'expulsion of the Manchus' at the top of its agenda. But in the larger historical picture nationalism was more important in being anti-imperialist **[Doc. 3, p. 119]**, making the British and other foreign powers a more significant, although less vulnerable, target of nationalist resentment. In this respect the Manchus were caught in a kind of catch-22. If they resisted the imperialists, they risked alienating the foreigners, whose support might well be crucial to their survival. On the other hand, if they failed to resist the imperialists, they would lose the loyalty of crucial sectors among their own subjects.

The other two of Sun Yat-sen's three principles of the people, democracy and people's livelihood, may have played a role in the success of the revolution. Democracy mattered in the sense that it was aimed against the Manchus and, after all, it was a republic that was founded. But the kind of democracy that mattered to groups like the provincial assemblies was not the kind Sun Yat-sen had in mind. And as for people's livelihood and the related notion of equal land rights and socialism, at this stage their influence was not particularly significant outside a group of intellectuals. Martin Bernal has written (in Wright, 1968: 141) that even for the revolutionaries 'interest in socialism of any sort was subordinate to their concern over national, constitutional, or even personal issues'.

The death of the Empress Dowager and the Guangxu Emperor at almost the same time had left a substantial vacuum of power at the centre, which nobody else could really fill. In other words, the Manchu dynasty was woefully lacking in leadership at its end. With a small boy as emperor, and no truly effective regents, there was nobody who could hold it together in a crisis. Reginald Johnston, tutor to Puyi from 1919 to 1924, judged the main Manchu leaders caustically, drawing the conclusion that their government 'was quickly reduced to a state bordering on imbecility' (Johnston, 1934: 83).

Meanwhile, the provincial assemblies were asserting their own authority at the expense of the central court. Even more important was the fact that many elements of the New Army turned against the dynasty that had created it and transferred their military power to the revolution. These assemblies and army included the most influential people within society, and the Manchu court could not afford to alienate them. This was a kind of class revolution, but it was certainly not a radical one in the Marxist sense. Scholars of the People's Republic of China have called it a 'bourgeois' revolution, but this interpretation is valid only in the sense that that the 'bourgeoisie' includes intellectuals, soldiers and members of the declining gentry among its members. It is true that the commercial bourgeoisie also turned against the Manchus, but their influence was not yet great enough to make them a crucial factor.

There were economic factors in the success of the revolution, especially serious natural disaster. As Mary Wright puts it, 'floods in Central China in the autumn of 1910 climaxed years of bad harvests' (1968: 49). Famine in the region became very serious, and threatened to get much worse as persistent rain intensified already widespread flooding. And there was a plague epidemic in Manchuria over the winter of 1910–11.

But three additional points need to be made about the Revolution of 1911, all of them negative in one sense or another. The first is that the small-picture reasons relating to such factors as natural disaster and the lack of support from the provincial assemblies pale into insignificance beside the big picture. This was that the Manchu dynasty had been in decline for well over a century. It had basically failed to cope with the problems of dynastic decline and of foreign imperialism. The Boxer Rebellion showed up its weakness with crystal clarity. What happened after that was that the Qing dynasty tried its best to restore itself through reform. These reforms were reasonably successful. But they could do no more than postpone the cataclysm, not prevent it altogether.

The second point is the relative lack of leadership on the revolutionary side. Though Sun Yat-sen is generally given credit for the revolution, 'he affected the chain of events that led China from the imperial monarchy to the Republic hardly at all' (Bergère, 1998: 245). He was not in China when the revolution broke out, resigned the presidency almost immediately on taking it over, and fled immediately from China on the failure of the 'Second Revolution'. As one noted biographer has pointed out, 'Behind the failure of this abortive revolution looms the failure of a leader who proved incapable of controlling, or even keeping up with the change for which he had yearned' (Bergère, 1998: 245).

The final point to note is related to the second. It is that in fact the Revolution of 1911 brought no radical transformation to the internal dynamics of Chinese society, and the structure of government remained essentially unchanged. Yuan Shikai was able to betray the revolution, robbing the revolutionaries of the fruits of their victory. In this sense one might even question whether this revolution fits the definition offered for the term in Chapter 1, which places the emphasis on radical change. But Yuan could not bring back the monarchy, and later attempts have also failed. The 1911 Revolution's main achievement of lasting importance was the overthrow of an imperial system that had endured for thousands of years. And that was in itself a change of proportions great enough to justify the term revolution.

5

Warlords, New Culture, 1916–28

The failure of Sun Yat-sen's revolution led on to a period of intense instability, perhaps the most pronounced feature of which was the rise of warlords. Most historians date the warlord period from 1916 to 1927–8, because the years when they dominated central government politics extended from Yuan Shikai's death in 1916 to Chiang Kai-shek's rise to power. However, in fact warlords held influence in some parts of China somewhat before 1915 and continued to do so, 'in a residual way, until 1937 and the Japanese invasion' (Bonavia, 1995: 2).

Partly as a result of the ideological vacuum following the collapse of the imperial system China experienced a new culture movement. This saw the rise of a generation of young people keen to overthrow the old traditions but at the same time intensely nationalistic and hostile to imperialism. Historians usually describe the whole process simply as the **May Fourth Movement**, after its centre-piece event, a major demonstration occurring on 4 May 1919.

May Fourth Movement: *Wusi yundong,* the process of intellectual, cultural and social revolution in China. The centerpiece event was a major demonstration on 4 May 1919: the May Fourth Incident.

THE WARLORD PERIOD

Several attempts have been made to define a warlord. James Sheridan (in Fairbank and Feuerwerker, 1983: XII, 284), in a simple, but adequate definition referring specifically to the period 1916–28 in China, describes a warlord as 'one who commanded a personal army, controlled or sought to control territory, and acted more or less independently'. Certainly these 'personal' armies took part in a great many wars, and Sheridan claims that there were 'literally hundreds of armed conflicts, short and long, on local, regional and national scales' over the years 1916 to 1928 (Fairbank and Feuerwerker, 1983: XII, p. 296).

The death of Yuan Shikai removed the only man capable of holding the nation together. Wrangling immediately broke out between the new President Li Yuanhong (1864–1928) and Premier Duan Qirui (1865–1936) over whether to enter the First World War against Germany. Duan Qirui, who favoured the move, put military pressure on the Parliament to support his view. Parliament responded by voting for Duan's resignation, so President Li Yuanhong dismissed him.

The warlord Zhang Xun, a man with very conservative, Confucian views, marched his army to Beijing, in theory to reinstate Duan but actually to restore the monarchy. He issued a manifesto arguing that the difference between a monarchy and republic was 'as great as the distance between heaven and earth' and that it was therefore his duty to attempt restoration **[Doc. 10, p. 125]**. On 1 July 1917 there was actually a coronation that restored the former Emperor Puyi to the throne.

Puyi's tenure of this high office was very short. On 7 July Duan Qirui's troops defeated Zhang's just outside Beijing. This was the first air raid in Chinese history, when an aeroplane from an aviation school outside Beijing actually bombed the Imperial Palaces. Duan, again premier, captured Beijing a few days later and forced Puyi from the throne.

Meanwhile, in September 1917, Sun Yat-sen founded the Military Government of the Republic of China, with its capital in Guangzhou in the south. Duan Qirui, wishing to reunite the country under his own rule, immediately sent troops against it. A bitter but indecisive north–south war broke out, lasting until towards the end of the following year.

The history of Sun's Guangzhou government will be considered in the next chapter. The northern forces split into several different cliques, with different interests and leaders, each trying to gain full control over the national government in Beijing. The main cliques were the Anfu, headed by Duan Qirui; the Zhili, led first by a succession of warlords, most notably Wu Peifu (1874–1939) (Wou, 1978); and the Fengtian or Manchurian clique, led by Zhang Zuolin (1875–1928) (McCormack, 1977).

In the summer of 1920 a short civil war between the Anfu and Zhili cliques took place, with the Fengtian clique siding with the Zhili and defeating Duan Qirui's forces. In 1922 Wu Peifu and Zhang Zuolin, having fought together against Duan, turned against each other for a second civil war. The outcome was that Zhang was driven back to Manchuria, leaving Wu in control of Beijing. However, in October and November 1924 a second Zhili–Fengtian civil war took place, but with a different result. Wu Peifu's ally, the warlord Feng Yuxiang (1882–1948) (Sheridan, 1966), turned against him, and Feng's troops occupied Beijing, expelling Wu and overthrowing the government his troops sponsored. Early in 1926 Zhang Zuolin formed another alliance with Wu Peifu against Feng Yuxiang, war breaking out immediately and resulting in the retreat of Feng's army from Beijing. These biennial northern civil wars were futile, even in their own terms, since it was Chiang Kai-shek whose forces eventually succeeded in reuniting the country.

FEATURES OF WARLORDS AND THEIR RULE

This last fact should alert us to one important factor of these unhappy years: the issue of national unity. Although the power bases of the warlords lay in specific regions, each man aimed to reunite the country, under his own control. Although they might fail in individual wars, focusing their attention on one area of the country, they were at one in recognising that there should be only one national government in China. The regional warlords controlled only one province or area, and could easily be all but independent of the rule of the central government. But that did not mean that they wished to set up an independent country separate from China. On the contrary, for all their personal power within their own domain, they knew that they were part of China.

Indeed, most of the warlords saw themselves as nationalists. Yet many were also strongly attached to foreign powers. Duan Qirui followed a very pro-Japanese policy, one factor seriously irritating most of his co-nationals. Wu Peifu had strong British connections and backing. A special case was Zhang Zuolin, a conservative without strong ideology but generally pro-Japanese. There was great irony in this fact, because Zhang actually met his death on 4 June 1928 at the hands of Japanese extremists, who blew up a train in which he was travelling. To Japan's intense irritation he had formed an alliance with the Nationalist Party earlier that year.

The warlords were power-hungry and, although some were certainly much more humane than others, most were cruel and self-indulgent as well. In his book on the warlords, David Bonavia (1995: 4) writes that they 'killed without compunction – their own men, if they breached discipline; the enemy's troops; often civilians if they resisted rape or plunder'. The cruellest of them was probably the Shandong warlord Zhang Zongchang, assassinated in September 1932 at the age of 50. His character comes through the phrase 'opening melons', which referred to his troops' frequent splitting of skulls. Sheridan (1975: 67–8) writes that, besides his rapacity and brutality, 'Zhang was known for his concubines and colourful personal habits. The number of his concubines has been variously reported between 30 and 50, although it is perhaps presumptuous of the historian to try to fix the number when Zhang himself allegedly did not know.'

Though the warlords had much in common, there were also strong differences among them. About 30 per cent of them could claim to be educated, the remainder being illiterate or semi-literate people of very humble origins. Of the dozen or so most prominent warlords, one had been a bandit, one a coolie, while two had risen from the rank of private.

They also differed in their ideologies. Some were ultra-conservative. A prime example was Zhang Xun, who briefly restored the monarchy. Another was Wu Peifu, a dedicated Confucianist and quite unconcerned about modern social reform, for instance suppressing with troops a major strike on the Beijing–Hankou railway in February 1923. But on the other hand, there were also warlords who spread social reform and adopted beliefs not traditional in China. By the standards of his day and country, Yan Xishan developed very good education and social welfare systems in Shanxi Province. Feng Yuxiang, 'the Christian general', was not only a firm believer himself but also, seeing his religion as a force for morale and discipline, attempted to spread it among his officers and men as well.

There have been a variety of judgements about the warlords and framework developed to analyse their rule. Hsi-sheng Ch'i (1976: 201–6) uses a balance-of-power framework for warlord politics, which views their activities and rivalries as similar to international relations. Another model, suggested by Lucien Pye, sees warlord rule as an unsuccessful attempt at modernization, because of the role of the military in a developing state as a modernizing agent. In this view, 'the warlords represented a high point in the development of a pluralistic and diversified power system in modern China' and on balance 'probably contributed more to the modernization of China than critics of their day recognized' (Pye, 1971: 168, 170). Both these views have their merits, but the frameworks underestimate the damaging effect of the constant war the period brought. They also suggest a somewhat more charitable impression about the warlords themselves than the realities might warrant. For the average Chinese citizen, the warlord period was an extremely miserable one, and, with some exceptions, the warlords' policies and activities merely exacerbated the desperation.

THE MAY FOURTH INCIDENT AND AFTERMATH

What actually happened on 4 May 1919, the date that gave its name to the famous and supremely important May Fourth Movement, was that about 3,000 students from Peking University, the most prestigious in China, and some dozen other educational institutions in the capital, marched from beneath the Tiananmen at the entrance to the Imperial Palaces to demonstrate against the foreign legations and the powers they represented. Turned away from the legation quarter by Chinese police and foreign guards, they marched instead to the residence of Minister of Communications Cao Rulin, a few students breaking into the house and setting it on fire. Other students beat up Chinese Minister to Japan Zhang Zongxiang. Thirty-two students were arrested and one student died later in hospital due to a violent clash with police.

The reason for the demonstration was that the Paris Peace Conference, which was working out the terms of a treaty to put a final end to the horrors of the First World War, had decided on 30 April 1919 to accept Japan's demands that all previously held German interests in Shandong Province should be handed over to Japan. This was despite the official Chinese position, backed by a mass rally in the Shandong capital Ji'nan on 20 April, that these interests should revert not to Japan but to China. The reason why Cao Rulin's residence was chosen for attack was because he had negotiated loans amounting to an enormous sum of money from Japan. In other words, the May Fourth Incident was in large measure aimed against Japan and its collaborators in Chinese leadership circles. The 'Manifesto of All the Students of Beijing' distributed during the demonstration focuses its attention on the Japanese demand and on China's territorial integrity [Doc. 11, p. 126].

Following the demonstrations in Beijing on 4 May, citizens' rallies took place in Shanghai and various other parts of China. The main issue in the protests was still the Paris decision on Shandong. They also called for the release of students arrested in Beijing. On 14 May the Beijing government issued a prohibition against student participation in politics, ordering the police to prevent public meetings. The failure of this action to curb escalating discontent was obvious from the fact that a general strike by tertiary students began five days later in Beijing, spreading quickly both to secondary students and to other cities. The demands of the strikers included a boycott on Japanese goods.

On 5 June further strikes occurred in Shanghai, spreading over the next few days to Wuhan, Tianjin, Ji'nan and other cities. What was significant about these protests was that the participants were not students but businessmen and workers. Their aim was to support the demands made by the students, including for the release of arrested students and the dismissal of the main pro-Japanese leadership. On 10 June, under this public pressure, the Beijing government dismissed Cao Rulin and Zhang Zongxiang from their posts. The strikers responded with a mass demonstration on 12 June, celebrating their victory but calling off all further workers' and business strikes.

The Treaty of Versailles was not actually signed until 28 June. As it turned out, the Chinese government was persuaded by the movement not to sign the treaty. However, the protests in China did not sway the powers from their decision on Shandong: under Articles 156–8 of the Treaty of Versailles Germany was forced to hand over all its rights in Shandong to Japan, China gaining nothing.

THE NEW CULTURE OR MAY FOURTH MOVEMENT

Although the term May Fourth Movement can apply simply to the trends touched off by the demonstration of 4 May 1919, it is more frequently used for the whole concatenation of progressive events and processes that made up the cultural and intellectual revolution of the few years following the Twenty-one Demands (see previous chapter) of 1915. This movement is also sometimes called the New Culture Movement.

One of the early intellectual driving forces of the New Culture Movement was a magazine edited by the prominent progressive **Chen Duxiu** in Shanghai (Feigon, 1983). First published in September 1915 under the title *Youth Magazine* (*Qingnian zazhi*), it was renamed *New Youth* (*Xin qingnian*) in September 1916. It published articles on social, literary and cultural matters, and became the mouthpiece for the progressive wing of the new movement.

One of the main ideological targets of *New Youth* was Confucianism. The magazine fiercely and unapologetically attacked everything associated with the Confucian tradition. It believed these traditions contrary to those forms of modernization necessary for the twentieth century. Instead, it advocated the introduction of 'two gentlemen' called Mr Science and Mr Democracy, who alone could save China **[Doc. 12, p. 126]**.

Traditionalists attacked the kind of ideas emerging from the New Culture Movement as treacherous and anti-Chinese. They saw Confucianism as part of the 'national essence' (*guocui*), which patriots should uphold. In some respects they were, of course, perfectly right. Confucianism was so closely associated with Chinese culture as to be almost synonymous with it. While China's tradition of science is very worthwhile and there are elements of democracy in Chinese culture, what *New Youth* was calling for was those forms of science or democracy that have become universally acknowledged as integral to the modern world.

The proponents of the new culture could see that many traditions were obstacles to China's advance into the modern world. Yet the new culturalists

Chen Duxiu (1879–1942): Progressive thinker and leader of the New Culture Movement. Leader of the founders of the Chinese Communist Party in May 1920, he was elected secretary-general at its First Congress in 1921 and removed in 1927. Imprisoned by the Nationalist Party government in 1932, and released on the outbreak of the War Against Japan.

considered themselves as very patriotic and nationalist. They saw themselves as the defenders of Chinese territorial integrity against onslaughts from the imperialists, especially Japan, and the conservatives who were in league with these forces.

As the May Fourth Movement developed, new and more modern and progressive trends appeared in virtually all branches of knowledge (Schwarcz, 1986). The Chinese looked at their own history in new ways, using forms of historiography introduced from the West. They departed from the traditional chronological way of recording the past, which they regarded as mere chronicles, and wrote works that were more thematic and analytical than what had come before. They felt that writing should avoid that kind of elevated style that meant nothing except to a highly educated class of men. The most radical faction wanted to abolish the use of Chinese characters altogether, because of their association with the Chinese tradition, but this view did not gain much support.

Although numerous figures emerged from the period, two at different poles of the ideological spectrum are of special interest. On the liberal wing was Hu Shi (1891–1962), discussed also in Chapter 13. Although he wrote in the vernacular and used literature to attack social problems, he opposed the left-wing thrust of the movement, and was very scornful of isms, such as socialism and anarchism. That the radical wing of the movement could indulge in such 'dream talk' he described as 'iron-clad proof of the bankruptcy of the Chinese intelligentsia . . . the death sentence for Chinese social reform' (Grieder, 1970: 124). In later years Hu became a fervent Nationalist Party supporter and went to live in Taiwan when the Chinese Communist Party (CCP) took over the mainland. On the left-wing end was **Lu Xun**, the best short-story writer modern China has produced, discussed in Chapter 13. His works show a fierce hostility to Chinese tradition and to all forms of class injustice, for which reason he has received strong commendation from the CCP.

Lu Xun (pen-name of Zhou Shuren, 1881–1936): Twentieth-century China's most famous writer. Famous especially for his socially satiric short stories, especially 'The True Story of A Q' ('A Q zhengzhuan'). Very left-wing in his sympathies, he won fulsome praise from Mao Zedong.

The New Culture and May Fourth Movement brought about other progressive trends in China. A few require mentioning here, because of their importance. However, they will be developed in greater detail in other chapters.

The first is that the May Fourth Movement produced the intellectual climate that facilitated the CCP's founding. Chen Duxiu was the leader of a group that secretly founded the party in Shanghai in May 1920. Li Dazhao (1888–1927) became the Chief Librarian at Peking University in February 1918, in that capacity appointing Mao Zedong (1893–1976) as assistant librarian the same year. Extremely left-wing in his thinking he exercised a profound influence on the young Mao. Zhang Zuolin's troops arrested him at the Soviet Embassy in Beijing in April 1927, and he was hanged the same month (Meisner, 1967).

In social terms the May Fourth Movement was significant in that it produced an added appreciation of the importance of women's rights. There was even a feminist wing among the New Culture thinkers. This was, in some respects, also a youth revolution, the first time in modern Chinese history that large-scale demonstrations of young people had taken place against the authorities. Such factors foreshadowed much more deep-seated social change over the coming decades, signalling this period's importance for China's transformation.

The May Fourth Movement adopted a new approach to literature. The proponents of the New Culture wanted literature to be written in the vernacular, so that it could be meaningful to ordinary people. May Fourth literature was much more focused on progressive social causes, such as upholding the value and rights of the downtrodden classes of society, the defence of Chinese national integrity and women's rights. Its style of written language abandoned the past classical idiom and tended much more towards contemporary usage.

6

The Nationalist Movement and Revolution

T he Guangzhou regime Sun Yat-sen set up in 1917 was the basis from which he made further attempts to launch a revolution to unite the whole of China under the Nationalist Party. Although he encountered many obstacles and died without achieving his aims, it was in his last years that he led the reorganization of the Nationalist Party and developed his three principles of the people most fully. In the end it was his fervent supporter Chiang Kai-shek who actually succeeded in leading the **Northern Expedition** from the southern city of Guangzhou and in reuniting the country under his leadership (see especially Fitzgerald, 1996 and Sheridan, 1975).

Northern Expedition: The military expedition sent north from Guangzhou to unite the country. The main and successful Northern Expedition was led by Chiang Kai-shek from 1926 to 1928.

THE GUANGZHOU REGIMES

Sun drew his support for the first Guangzhou regime – formally the Republic of China (ROC) Military Government – from former members of the National Assembly that Yuan Shikai had dissolved early in 1914. His explicit aims were to oppose the warlord Beijing government and revive the constitution. To this end he organized a 'protect the constitution' campaign which, despite the vigour and enthusiasm he gave it, never really got off the ground.

Just as in his earlier revolution, Sun's government was made up of very disparate elements. Local warlords and businessmen dominated, with Sun's main supporters making up only a part. In May 1918 the National Assembly reorganized the Military Government, the effect being to reduce Sun Yat-sen's power greatly and hand it over to warlords. Following serious power struggle among the leadership, Sun even formally disbanded this ROC Military Government in mid-1920.

Later in 1920 Sun set up a second Guangzhou regime, and had himself elected Extraordinary President of the ROC the following May. Again the main aim was to oppose the warlords. In February 1922 Sun issued orders for a 'Northern Expedition' to defeat the warlords and unite the country, but he had to call it off in July.

What finally put paid to this attempt was Sun's quarrel with the local warlord Chen Jiongming (1878–1933), a former supporter and theoretically his subordinate. Sun tried to patch up his fight with Chen Jiongming, who responded by ordering a military attack on Sun's presidential palace in Guangzhou in mid-June 1922. Sun narrowly escaped to a warship in the Pearl River on which Guangzhou lies, sailing to Shanghai. Not until mid-January 1923 did mercenaries loyal to Sun actually retake Guangzhou from Chen Jiongming.

Sun's attempts to create a regime alternative to the warlords, let alone one that could defeat them, were obviously very weak. However, in Shanghai he was enthusiastically received. At the beginning of January 1923 his Nationalist Party adopted its constitution in Shanghai, with Sun's three principles of the people as the ideological basis. To cap these factors, Sun gained something he had wanted for some time: diplomatic recognition.

The major Western powers had been very critical of Sun Yat-sen, regarding him as a idealistic dreamer. Certainly they were not prepared to give him any economic aid. Sun's ideas had been drifting significantly to the left, including a strong emphasis on anti-imperialism. At the time the Soviet Union was still an international pariah and, like Sun, very keen for foreign support. In Shanghai Sun met with the Soviet diplomatic delegate in Beijing, Adolph Joffe who, having failed in an attempt to negotiate a treaty with the warlord government, was keen to deal with Sun. On 26 January 1923 the two signed a joint communique **[Doc. 13, p. 127]**. Among several provisions, two were of particular value to Sun:

- the Soviet Union would assist in China's reunification;
- both parties agreed that communism was not applicable to China.

'Sun behaved as a head of state and, with the signature that he placed at the foot of the document, Joffe granted him that status' (Bergère: 1998, 310). The Soviet Union thus became the first foreign power to do so. The acknowledgement that communism was inapplicable to China seemed to strengthen Sun's hand vis-à-vis the Chinese Communist Party (CCP).

THE FIRST CONGRESS OF THE NATIONALIST PARTY; SUN'S THREE PRINCIPLES OF THE PEOPLE

Sun returned to Guangzhou in February 1923 and there became generalissimo of a new Guangzhou government, one of his chief appointments being Chiang Kai-shek as chief-of-staff. Despite further armed conflict with Chen Jiongming and other warlords later in the year, Sun was able at this time to strengthen his forces politically and to reorganize the Nationalist Party. One person who helped him enormously in this endeavour was Soviet emissary Michael Borodin, who had close links to Lenin and other Soviet leaders; Sun even appointed him formal adviser. Partly because of Borodin's role, but also because of a crisis in which interested foreign powers sent gunboats to prevent Sun's regime from taking over the Guangzhou customs house, the Nationalist Party moved increasingly to the left and became more strident in its anti-imperialist rhetoric.

This was reflected in the First Congress of the Nationalist Party, which ran from 20 to 30 January 1924, though with three days' adjournment to mourn Lenin's death (21 January). The party proclamation stressed hostility to imperialism and militarism but support for mass participation in the national revolution, especially of poor peasants and workers. Since the Nationalist Party had just formed a united front with the CCP, some of the delegates were members of both parties. One counter to these signs of left-wing influence was that Borodin tried, but failed, to persuade Sun 'to include a clear statement of the movement's united front with Soviet Russia' (Wilbur, 1984: 11). Sun gave seven speeches altogether, including the opening address, which called for unity and sacrifice among party members. He also tried to get a statement into the proclamation supporting radical land reform. But in fact what emerged was more a reformist programme, based on solving China's problems through moderate measures, than a revolutionary one.

Sun Yat-sen's three principles of the people – nationalism, democracy and people's livelihood – were now firmly entrenched in Nationalist Party ideology, their most detailed articulation being in several lectures Sun gave in 1924. In contrast to the earlier part of his career, nationalism was now no longer directed against the Manchus (see Chapter 4), since the Manchu dynasty had now been overthrown. Instead, nationalism was directed against the Western powers and Japan **[Doc. 14, p. 127]**. Sun's concern about the notion of the state is also noteworthy. He refers to the doctrine of the state-nation (*guozu zhuyi*) **[Doc. 15, p. 128]**, bemoaning China's inability to overcome attachment to family in favour of country. What is clear is the imprint of Sun's experiences in attempting to carry out a revolution.

The same can be said about the second principle, democracy, or the power of the people **[Doc. 16, p. 129]**. Sun's emphasis here is on equality and on peace. Bitterness against the failure of the Republic, warlord power and monarchist restoration attempts is obvious in Sun's notion. But at the same time he is quite right to point to the progress inherent in the fact that 'the average great military man of today does not dare to call himself a prince or petty one to become a marquis'.

The third principle, that of people's livelihood, shows the extent to which Sun Yat-sen had moved to the left late in his life. In his lecture of 3 August 1924, Sun has much to say in praise of Karl Marx and his system of socialism, and acknowledges Marxist influence over his own thinking **[Doc. 17, p. 130]**. However, he also attacks the doctrine of class struggle, and the last paragraph of the lecture shows Sun's disagreement with the central tenet of Marxism, that economic mode of production is the determining factor in world history.

Considering the difficulties Sun and his colleagues faced, among which warlord opposition was paramount, the reorganization and First Congress of the Nationalist Party was a remarkable achievement. However, it was also among his last. In January 1925 he went to Beijing for various reasons, including treatment of suspected cancer of the liver, of which he died on 12 March 1925. He had declared in his last will, written on 20 February, that the work of the people's revolution, to which he had devoted himself for forty years, was 'not yet done' (Sun, 1927: vii). Sun's career had indeed been full of disappointments. Yet the fact remains that he is one of the very few leaders of modern China whom Chinese of virtually all political persuasions can agree to admire.

THE RISE OF CHIANG KAI-SHEK; THE NORTHERN EXPEDITION BEGINS

Shortly after its First Congress the Nationalist Party established a military academy in Whampoa to the south of Guangzhou. The academy relied heavily on advice from Borodin and aimed to train junior officers who would be both competent and totally loyal to the Nationalist Party and its ideology. The man whom Sun Yat-sen chose to appoint as commandant of the newly opened academy was Chiang Kai-shek. Very soon after he played a leading role in reorganizing the Guangzhou army, under the name **National Revolutionary Army (NRA)**. He also determined to carry out Sun Yat-sen's wish for a Northern Expedition, which would overthrow the northern

National Revolutionary Army (NRA): The name of Chiang Kai-shek's army in his Northern Expedition, formed in 1925.

warlords and reunite all China under a government led by the Nationalist Party.

Born to a middle-level rural family in Zhejiang Province in October 1887, Chiang had received military training in Japan before the 1911 Revolution and then actually joined the Imperial Japanese Army for a period. After return to China he joined Sun Yat-sen's Guangzhou regime in the south, and was sent to Moscow to study the Soviet Red Army. His primary loyalty was to Sun Yat-sen himself and, although his ambitions for leadership were not in doubt, his political attitude towards the left-wing drift of the Nationalist Party in Sun's last days was not clear.

However, in November 1925, ten right-wing members of the Nationalist Party's leading body, the Central Executive Council, held a meeting in the Western Hills just outside Beijing. This group, which came to be known as the Western Hills Clique, took a decision to eliminate all Communist influence within the party. It called for the expulsion of all CCP members who had joined the Nationalist Party under the policy of the united front and demanded that the leading leftist figure within the party, Wang Jingwei (1883–1944), be punished.

The Nationalist Party held its Second Congress in January 1926 in Guangzhou. It rejected the Western Hills meeting as invalid. It elected a Central Executive Council of thirty-six, including Wang Jingwei, Chiang Kai-shek, Hu Hanmin (1879–1936) and even the Communist Li Dazhao, and a nine-man Standing Committee dominated by leftists. The Congress thus represented a significant victory for the left.

This triumph was very short-lived. Just two months after the Congress ended, Chiang Kai-shek carried out a minor coup against the left through the *Zhongshan* Incident. What specifically happened was that he seized the gunboat *Zhongshan*, which was lying off his headquarters at the Whampoa Academy, and arrested its communist captain, Li Zhilong, declared martial law in Guangzhou and ordered his troops to disarm guards protecting the Soviet advisers' residences. Why he took this sudden action is unclear. Martin Wilbur suggests his reasons might have included hostility towards three of the top Soviet military advisers 'because of their domineering attitudes' and refusal to support his plans for a Northern Expedition. Chiang may also have been led to believe from the suspicious movements of the *Zhongshan* 'that a plan to abduct him and send him to Russia was underway' (Wilbur, 1984: 47).

The *Zhongshan* Incident certainly signalled a dramatic turn to the right. As the leader of the left-wing faction within the Nationalist Party, Wang Jingwei felt under threat and went into hiding, shortly afterwards going to France. However, Chiang Kai-shek retained the services of the Soviet advisers and curbed the power of the far right within the party in a bid to keep the united front with the CCP intact.

In June the National Government appointed Chiang as NRA commander-in-chief and the next month he assumed the position of chairman of the Central Executive Committee. In July the Northern Expedition began, gaining early successes and taking the capital of Hunan Province, Changsha, with little opposition. Wu Peifu decided to resist in Hubei Province, just north of Hunan, and the NRA faced stiff opposition from warlord-controlled troops in several other areas. Nevertheless, by the end of 1926 the NRA had taken the capitals and major cities of Hunan, Hubei, Jiangxi and Fujian, as well as holding the original base of Guangdong and adding Guangxi to its west through negotiation. In other words, the Nationalist Revolution had taken more or less the whole of the southeast of China. Moreover, the National Government had moved its headquarters north to the main city of Hubei, Wuhan, which it formally declared its national capital on 1 January 1927.

THE SPLIT IN THE REVOLUTION; CHIANG KAI-SHEK'S SHANGHAI COUP

The advance of the NRA was accompanied by strong radical influences, including anti-imperialism and an upsurge in the Communist-inspired labour movement (Chesneaux, 1968). In Wuhan the Hubei General Labour Union, formed in October 1926, claimed a membership of over 300,000. Early in January 1927, just after the capital had moved to the city, anti-British feeling flared into mob violence demanding the return of the British Concession in Hankou. The British government, which had abandoned its policy of gunboat diplomacy in 1925, opted for conciliation, as a result of which British Concessions both in Hankou and in Jiujiang, Jiangxi Province, were handed back to the Chinese in March. These developments are interesting and important not only for their role in the Nationalist Revolution, but also because they represented the first stage of British imperial retreat from China (see Fung, 1991: 105–28).

The NRA took both Nanjing and Shanghai towards the end of March 1927. Foreign hostility to the Nationalists was exacerbated by the fact that Nationalist troops systematically looted the British, American and Japanese consulates on 24 March and attacked and robbed foreigners throughout the city. The workers and leftists, on the other hand, were delighted by the NRA's successes. In Shanghai they had already begun an armed revolution, including setting up a workers' government and organizing major strikes, but been suppressed by warlord troops. They greeted the NRA enthusiastically as liberators.

Their joy was short-lived. On 12 April Chiang Kai-shek carried out a large-scale anti-CCP coup in Shanghai, beginning massive purges against the left and the labour movement. The following day his troops suppressed an enormous demonstration of many thousands of workers and a general strike held in Shanghai. Troops fired at the demonstrators, killing over 100 and wounding many more. The NRA, which the workers had welcomed with such enthusiasm in Shanghai not long before, had turned against them with a vengeance.

The CCP, the Soviet Union and the left of the Nationalist Party were naturally alarmed at this turn of events, obviously very much more dramatic in its implications than the *Zhongshan* Incident of March 1926. However, they were not prepared to give up. On 1 April Wang Jingwei returned from Europe and four days later he and CCP leader Chen Duxiu issued a joint statement calling for the continuation of the united front between the Nationalist Party and CCP. When Chiang set up his National Government in Nanjing in April, Wang Jingwei remained in Wuhan at the head of a left government there. At its Fifth Congress, held in Hankou from 27 April to 5 May 1927, the CCP decided to continue the united front with Wang Jingwei, but oppose Chiang Kai-shek. A week after the end of the Congress, Chiang's government announced that it would attempt the total elimination of its Wuhan rival. The revolution was thus rent asunder.

But again this situation proved temporary and to the detriment of the left. Christian warlord Feng Yuxiang threw his weight behind Chiang Kai-shek's wish to reunite the country, but against the left and the other warlords. In June he held meetings both with Wang Jingwei and Chiang Kai-shek, offering his good offices to heal the rift between the two leaders. The upshot of the meeting with Wang was the latter's agreement to curb Communist influence; the Feng–Chiang meeting resulted in a joint communique expressing determination to complete the Northern Expedition. Feng Yuxiang immediately cabled Wang Jingwei urging unity with Chiang Kai-shek and opposition to the CCP.

Wang proved receptive to this appeal. Despite being cheered by a meeting of the All-China Labour Federation on 23 June, his troops moved in to suppress the General Trade Union at the end of the month. In July he stepped up military attacks on trade unions, confiscating archives and property in a systematic, and successful, attempt to destroy the labour movement in Hubei. In the middle of July he began savage suppression of the CCP in Hubei, with the result that Borodin and other Soviet advisers of the Wuhan government left for home at the end of the month. The united front between the Nationalist Party and the CCP was over.

The following months saw the further destruction of the CCP and the left in the cities, with very large numbers of people killed in the process. The

Northern Expedition continued, although with some resistance, notably from the Japanese, who seized the Shandong capital Ji'nan from the NRA in May. Despite such setbacks, the NRA took both Beijing and Tianjin in June. At the end of 1928 the ruler of Manchuria **Zhang Xueliang**, who had taken over on the assassination of his father Zhang Zuolin in the middle of the year, formally pledged the loyalty of the northeast provinces to the National Government. This action signalled the success of the Northern Expedition and the reunification of the country under the National Government of Chiang Kai-shek.

Zhang Xueliang (1901–2001): Succeeded his father as northeast Chinese warlord in 1928, then submitted to Chiang Kai-shek, signalling the reunification of China on the Northern Expedition's completion. He kidnapped Chiang in 1936, forcing him to resist Japan. Chiang immediately arrested Zhang Xueliang who spent most of the rest of his life under house arrest in Taiwan.

7

The Nanjing Decade, 1927–37

Nanjing decade: The ten years from Nanjing's establishment as the capital of Chiang Kai-shek's National Government to the outbreak of the War Against Japan: 1927–37.

The **Nanjing decade** is the term applied to the period beginning when Nanjing became the capital of China in 1927 and ending with the outbreak of the War of Resistance Against Japan, or Second Sino-Japanese War, in 1937. The period was not without its accomplishments, and its final years saw the best economic conditions in China of any period under consideration in this book. At the same time, Chiang Kai-shek's National Government faced stiff opposition from several domestic and foreign quarters. Above all, the Japanese were a constant threat to Chiang's China (Eastman, 1974) Doc. 20 gives an assessment of the period **[Doc. 20, p. 132]**.

POLITICS AND THE STRUGGLE AGAINST OPPOSITION

Despite his success in leading the Northern Expedition, Chiang Kai-shek still faced very substantial opposition. Even apart from the CCP, to be considered in greater detail in the next chapter, there was very substantial leftist influence within the ruling Nationalist Party. Some of the warlords remained a powerful force, with the potential to destabilize his government. And Japan had shown it was able and willing to assert itself at China's expense.

Chiang Kai-shek saw his first task as purging the Nationalist Party of leftists. By the time of the Third Nationalist Party Congress, March 1929, the right wing was totally dominant. Chiang Kai-shek had placed his supporters in all the main positions, disciplined leaders of the left wing, and imposed his own ideas on the party and government. Among the most important of these was a theory of stages of government focused on a notion of political tutelage (discussed in a later section).

In January 1929 Chiang Kai-shek held a National Reorganization and Demobilization Conference in Nanjing, attended by the country's principal military figures and warlords, including Feng Yuxiang and Yan Xishan. The Conference agreed to trim the various armies of China, which currently numbered about 2 million, to 800,000 and to cut military spending. However, Chiang's real aim was to reduce rival armies, not his own, and the Conference actually exacerbated the warlords' suspicions of Chiang and their hostility towards him (Eastman et al., 1991: 10–11).

The result was a series of civil wars. The most serious of them lasted for several months in 1930 and saw Chiang Kai-shek pitted against a coalition including Feng Yuxiang and Yan Xishan, supported even by members of Chiang's own government, notably Wang Jingwei. Chiang won the war, partly because of major military support from the Manchurian warlord Zhang Xueliang. But the cost was heavy, for this was an extremely destructive war causing physical devastation to the affected territories and a total of some 250,000 casualties.

Another major rebellion broke out in Fujian from mid-December 1933, lasting a month. The governor of Fujian, Chen Mingshu, declared the province independent and proclaimed the establishment of the People's Revolutionary Government. 'The chief target of the rebellion was Chiang Kai-shek, whom the rebels denounced for neglect of popular welfare, failure to implement democracy, and inadequate responses to Japanese encroachments on China' (Sheridan, 1975: 192). The rebels had expected support both from several of the warlords and the Communists in Jiangxi (see Chapter 8). In the event, however, they got very little backing and were massively defeated by Chiang's troops.

These are but two examples of a range of civil wars, apart from a series against the Communists, which Chiang Kai-shek faced during the Nanjing decade. It is true that the situation improved for political and economic reasons from September 1936 and into the following year, one authority even stating the 'a new sense of optimism and national unity suffused the nation' (Eastman et al., 1991: 45) at that time. But the reality is that, apart from the provinces around and nearest the capital, especially Jiangsu and Zhejiang, Chiang Kai-shek's hold over China's territory was generally somewhat tenuous and he faced military and political opposition from many quarters for virtually the whole decade.

The foreign country of greatest concern to Chiang Kai-shek's regime was Japan. The struggle against Japan will be the main focus of Chapter 9. Here it must be mentioned that the Japanese invaded Manchuria in 1931, setting up a puppet state there the following year, which they called Manchukoku. They placed on the throne the former Qing Emperor Puyi, but retained strict control over developments through a variety of mechanisms including military occupation. In May 1933 China signed a truce with Japan in the coastal town of Tanggu, just east of Tianjin, ceding the northeast to Japan. Despite the Tanggu Truce, the Japanese continued to encroach towards the south and into Inner Mongolia, both militarily and politically. From January to May 1932 they occupied Shanghai, in theory to protect their own nationals.

Chiang Kai-shek temporized in reacting to the Japanese. He was so pre-occupied with the struggle against internal enemies and putative opponents that he did not even see the threat from Japan as the gravest China had to face. In a speech given in Fuzhou in April 1933, Chiang Kai-shek made the famous statement that 'the state's greatest worry is not so much the dwarf-pirates [Japanese] as Jiangxi's local bandits [the CCP]' (quoted Mackerras, 1982: 346). This view was not shared by most Chinese, especially the intel-ligentsia, who deeply resented Chiang's Japan policy (see also Chapter 12). Early in 1935 the Japanese made an overture of peace towards China, expressing the hope that anti-Japanese agitations would end. Wang Jingwei, at the time the Minister of Foreign Affairs, responded on 20 February by arguing that mutual sincerity and righteousness would bring about 'a rational solution of fundamental issues between the two countries'. He added that this 'will be a blessing not only for the two countries and for Eastern Asia, but it will be a blessing to the peace of the world' (Kwei, 1935–6: I, 378). Considering what happened later, there is deep and bitter irony in these words.

GOVERNMENT, PARTY

The National Government itself was composed of five bodies, known in Chinese as *yuan*. Literally the term means court, as in law court, house, as in House of Commons, or public building. But since it is essentially untranslat-able in the context of the branches of Nationalist Chinese government, most scholarly and other works simply use the original Chinese term.

The five bodies were (i) the Executive Yuan; (ii) the Legislative Yuan; (iii) the Judicial Yuan; (iv) the Examination Yuan; and (v) the Censor Yuan. The main functions of the first three are obvious from their title. The Examination Yuan attended to the selection of civil service candidates by examination and to the registration of persons qualified for public service. The Censor Yuan attended to impeachment and auditing.

Chiang Kai-shek's model of administration, as adopted in 1929, was bor-rowed from Sun Yat-sen and presupposed a three-stage process leading to constitutional government. After military occupation there would be a period of political tutelage, the principal aim of which was to create the time and opportunity to educate people in the theory and practice of democracy and constitutional government. Because the Chinese people had very little knowledge or experience of democracy, it was pointless to introduce it without detailed preparations **[Doc. 19, p. 131]**. Following the end of military occupation, Chiang's 1929 intention was to complete the period of tutelage by 1935. However, he believed it necessary that order must be completely restored in an individual province before political tutelage gave way to constitutional government. The Legislative Yuan adopted a draft constitution in October 1934, which was revised in 1936, but was not implemented, due to the outbreak of the War Against Japan.

One point of interest about the operation of democracy, as Chiang Kai-shek's government envisaged it, was that it should begin through self-government at the district and county levels, in other words from the localities towards the centre. On the other hand, it was the centre that should carry out education in self-government. To that end the central government would send out 'trained officers' to teach people at lower levels about such matters as completing a census and organizing a police force. Under Chiang Kai-shek's regime, Sun Yat-sen's principle of democracy meant that, 'the government should undertake to train and guide them [the people] so that they may know how to exercise their rights of election, recall, initiative, and referendum' (Kwei, 1935–6: I, 139).

The ideological basis of the Nationalist Party under Chiang Kai-shek remained Sun Yat-sen's three principles of the people. Chiang Kai-shek himself gave these principles his strong endorsement. In one passage he relates the three to human emotions (nationalism), law (democracy) and reason (people's livelihood), advocating them as the most appropriate ideological basis for human development. He also dismisses the notion, popular in his day (and in the twenty-first century) that the Chinese as a people are interested only in the rule of man, not of law. His evidence is the functions he finds for law in the three principles of the people **[Doc. 18, p. 130]**.

Other than members of the army, who were automatically listed as members, there were, in total, 324,038 Nationalist Party members in China itself, and 101,834 probational members in September 1934 (Kwei, 1935–6: I, 147). According to James Sheridan (1975: 214), less than half China's provinces had established regular party committees by 1933, and less than 18 per cent of counties had party branches, most of them in the provinces of the Yangzi Valley. 'In other words, party organizational strength went only as far as Chiang's bayonets', being especially weak in the countryside.

CORRUPTION, CHIANG KAI-SHEK'S POWER BASE

Notwithstanding the existence of the Censor Yuan within the government, the fact is that corruption was an abiding feature of Chiang Kai-shek's rule. Although it worsened considerably after the War Against Japan, it was already very serious during the Nanjing decade. Nepotism and bribery were rife among the bureaucracy and, in September 1936, Chiang Kai-shek himself stated: 'If we do not weed the present body of corruption, bribery, perfunctoriness, and ignorance, and establish instead a clean and efficient administration, the day will soon come when the revolution will be started against us as we did against the Manchus' (quoted Eastman et al., 1991: 49 **[Doc. 20, p. 132]**).

Corruption was actually much more serious than he acknowledged. Chiang Kai-shek's power rested less on the government, or even the Nationalist Party as a whole, as on his control of a very significant army and the financial world of Shanghai, and on certain factions within the Nationalist Party. Chiang's was not the only army in China, but it was the strongest and most important. His military background and experience in the Whampoa Military Academy and in developing the National Revolutionary Army gave him enormous power and prestige. In the days before 1927, Chiang had also developed very good contacts with the financial community of Shanghai, and quite possibly also with the Green Gang, a secret society with control over the underworld. During the Nanjing decade, Chiang and the Shanghai financiers depended on each other for support, Chiang knowing that he could outsmart any rivals through his contacts in this crucial field.

There were numerous factions within the Nationalist Party. Two worthy of mention here, for the control Chiang could exercise over them, were the CC Clique and the Whampoa Clique. The first of these was probably called after the two Chens, that is Chen Guofu and Chen Lifu, both close friends of Chiang Kai-shek. Through their control over the Organization Department of the Nationalist Party, they were able to place supporters in relevant positions, in particular in the party and government apparatus, educational agencies, youth organizations, trade unions and one of Chiang's two secret police organizations. The Whampoa Clique consisted mainly of military officers, especially graduates from the Whampoa Military Academy. Its main operational organization was a highly disciplined group called the Blue Shirts. Strongly influenced by the fascist doctrines of Nazi Germany, it became extremely powerful during the 1930s, not only within the army but even within civilian institutions such as schools and the police. The Blue Shirts also operated a secret police organization that carried out intelligence against anybody Chiang Kai-shek believed was an enemy, and was not above political assassinations.

According to Lloyd Eastman, 'The regime that took shape in Chiang Kai-shek's hands after 1927 was neither totalitarian nor democratic, but lay uncertainly between those points on the political spectrum' (Eastman et al., 1991: 19). Although the Nationalist Party and the government structure clearly remained important, Chiang Kai-shek was concerned that power should reside in his own hands and those of his main supporters, especially within the factions and army. The judgement of one historian is that 'Even allowing for the exigencies of the time and the necessity for firm leadership, Chiang Kai-shek's autocratic desires seemed inordinate' (McAleavy, 1967: 272). Eastman writes that the party, 'atrophied even more than did the governmental administration as a result of Chiang Kai-shek's transformation of the revolutionary movement into a military-authoritarian regime' (Eastman et al., 1991: 21). Perhaps not totalitarian, it was certainly corrupt and oppressive.

POPULATION

Some Chinese figures for China's population in selected years are given in Doc. 21 [Doc. 21, p. 133]. All these figures included the Manchurian provinces lost to Japan in 1931. They show the total as approximately 450 million in the mid-1930s. Also given are some figures for sex ratios, that is the number of males for every hundred females within the population, for selected years.

John Lossing Buck, whose work on land utilization in China is generally regarded as authoritative, claims that the sex ratio in China overall in 1929–31 was 108 (Buck, 1937: 375–6). He also adds a figure for the sex ratio at birth: 112.6 (Buck, 1937: 382–3). His figures for overall sex ratios are considerably lower than those given by the Chinese accounts quoted above, but still high enough to demand explanation, his suggestions including 'less complete enumeration of females than males' and higher female mortality. Some of this 'higher female mortality' was undoubtedly due to the ancient and traditionally quite widespread practice of female infanticide.

Despite their apparent precision, the figures given in Doc. 21 cannot be taken as more than approximate. But two points appear to emerge from them. One is that, for all its instability, the Republican period was a period of rising population until the outbreak of the War Against Japan. The other is that the sex ratio fell slightly over the period, but remained high, with a significant preponderance of males over females.

THE ECONOMY

The early years of the Nanjing decade saw serious drought-famine in the northwestern provinces, especially Gansu and Shaanxi, with several million deaths. Flooding along the Yangzi River in 1931 saw waters in Hankou reach their highest point since records were first taken in the 1860s. Economically speaking, the Nanjing decade got off to a very bad start.

As a result of the worldwide depression of the late 1920s and early 1930s, the price of China's exports to the West fell significantly. When the West recovered, imports rose, silver poured out of China, and the banks lost reserves. The result was that some banks were put out of business while the lack of cash pushed some industrial firms to bankruptcy.

However, in the years 1935–7 economic conditions improved greatly. Production of rice, wheat and other commodities rose, with bumper harvests. The government carried out a currency reform, which consisted mainly of abandoning the silver standard. Agricultural prices rose, with credit becoming more readily available. The improvement in the countryside gave impetus also for growth of the urban economy.

The Nanjing decade saw some improvements in China's communications. Postal and telephone services expanded significantly, and air routes increased. The total length of highways had grown to 115,702 kilometres by 1937, of which 40,218 were surfaced (Chinese Ministry of Information, 1944: 148). There was growth also in the railway system, with 1936 seeing the completion of the very important Guangzhou–Hankou line.

China generally remained very poor for most people, with great variations between regions and classes. Buck's data from a variety of areas over the period 1929 to 1933, but specifically avoiding famine regions, gives a generally positive picture, with the claim that 'the food energy consumption of the country as a whole is markedly above the standard' calorie intake (Buck, 1937: 408). On the other hand, Eastman, noting that China's death rate was among the highest in the world, markedly higher even than India's, observes that 'farmers lived in appalling poverty, a year of sickness or poor weather plunging them over the edge of subsistence' (Eastman et al., 1991: 36).

Landlordism was a serious problem in some parts of China, being generally much worse in the rice-growing south than the wheat-growing north. The most extensive survey on this matter, that carried by the National Government's National Agricultural Research Bureau and published in 1935, showed that 44 per cent of farmers owned their land, 23 per cent were part-owners, and 33 per cent tenants (Buck, 1937: 195–6). These figures may not support the dire picture painted by the left, and after all landlordism was hardly unique to China. But they did suggest serious inequality and poverty in many areas.

There has been considerable controversy over how to evaluate the extent of modernization in the Chinese economy. Chinese scholars of the post-Mao period have tended to a more positive view than they had done earlier. They tend to argue, in Tim Wright's words, that 'the Chinese bourgeoisie had major achievements to its credit' and that 'the statistical record of the modern sector up to 1936 shows substantial growth, both of total output and of the Chinese-owned sector' (Wright, 1992: 13). On the other hand, Eastman points out that only about 3.4 per cent of the net domestic product lay in the modern sector of manufacturing, mining and utilities (Eastman et al., 1991: 36).

China's economic performance over this period was thus very mixed. The standard of living remained low or extremely low for most of the people, especially the 90 per cent or so who lived in the villages. On the other hand, there was definitely some growth, and the persistent poverty should not divert some credit from Chiang Kai-shek's regime in the economic sphere.

8

The Chinese Communist Party

Born in the shadow of the May Fourth Movement, the Chinese Communist Party (CCP) played a very important role in the nationalist movement of the 1920s because of its united front with the Nationalist Party. After its suppression in 1927 the CCP went underground, founding its own Chinese Socialist Republic in Jiangxi Province in 1931. Chiang Kai-shek expended considerable military effort to destroy this republic. His success in this venture, however, drove the CCP to their famous Long March, which took them to a new headquarters in northern Shaanxi Province at the other end of China. It was there that they created a new model of revolution, also adopting a major role in resisting the Japanese (Guillermarz, 1972; Harrison, 1973; Saich, 1996).

THE EARLY PERIOD

Though Chen Duxiu had formed the CCP initially in 1920, the First Congress was not held until July 1921. There were thirteen Chinese delegates present, representing just under sixty members, and the Dutch agent Maring of the Communist International or Comintern (pseudonym of H. Sneevliet). Zhang Guotao took the chair, while Mao Zedong represented Hunan Province. Although absent, Chen Duxiu was elected secretary-general. The meeting began in Shanghai's French Concession, but, because of suspicious activities leading the delegates to believe themselves under threat, it moved to a boat on a lake in nearby Zhejiang Province.

The Congress took two main decisions. One was that the CCP was a party of the proletariat and should involve itself actively in the labour movement. The other was that the CCP should cooperate with Sun Yat-sen and his

Guangzhou regime, while at the same time remaining critical of his teachings. The Second Congress, which took place in July 1922 in Shanghai, resolved to form a united front with the Nationalist Party against imperialism and the warlords, and to join the Comintern.

In June 1923 the CCP, with 432 members, held its Third Congress in Guangzhou. In class terms it lay stress on the interests of workers and peasants. It formally declared that the Nationalist Party 'should be the central force of the national revolution and should assume its leadership' (quoted Brandt, Schwartz and Fairbank, 1971: 71). At the same time it adopted Lenin's 'bloc within' strategy, which meant that it wished to retain its own organization and structure at the same time as it entered into a united front with the Nationalist Party. Later the same year, Michael Borodin, becoming adviser to Sun Yat-sen, convinced doubters both in the Nationalist Party and CCP of the united front's benefits.

So when the First Nationalist Party Congress met in Guangzhou in January 1924, there were delegates belonging both to the CCP and Nationalist Parties. Three senior CCP members, including Li Dazhao, were actually elected to the Nationalist Party's Central Executive Committee, while Mao Zedong, a member of the CCP's Central Committee, became an alternate. Li Dazhao made a speech emphasising the CCP delegates' loyalty to the national revolution and disclaiming any wish to infiltrate the Nationalist Party for subversive purposes (Dirlik, 1989; Meisner, 1967; Saich, 1991).

One of the most striking features of the earliest CCP period was the development of a peasant movement in the southern provinces, especially Guangdong and Hunan. As early as May 1922, Peng Pai, a CCP member though from a rich family, had begun organizing a peasant revolution in his native Haifeng County, a thickly populated area of southeastern Guangdong. He gained substantial early successes, inaugurating the Haifeng Federation of Peasant Unions on 1 January 1923, with a membership of some 20,000.

By far the most famous peasant movement was that in Hunan, in which Mao Zedong was closely involved. As early as 1919, Mao had written an article, putting forward the idea that the Chinese could rescue themselves from their misery only by arising in a powerful union, the first groups he mentioned being peasants and workers **[Doc. 22, p. 134]**. Early in 1927 he wrote his now famous 'Report on an Investigation of the Peasant Movement in Hunan' **[Doc. 23, p. 134]**. The Wuhan National Government expressed concern at excesses within the peasant movement, but Mao was exuberant over its success and potential for leadership of the revolution. Although the events of 1927 did not bear out his optimism, the experience laid the foundation for more successful peasant involvement in the revolution later on (Payne, 1950; Schram, 1966).

THE END OF THE UNITED FRONT AND AFTERMATH

When Chiang Kai-shek and even Wang Jingwei turned against the CCP (see Chapter 6), it was forced to change immediately from a party of government to one of insurrection. At the beginning of August 1927 several CCP leaders staged an uprising in Nanchang, the capital of Jiangxi Province. The attempt proved disastrous, with the city held for only five days, but did enter CCP mythology in the sense that 1 August 1927 is still regarded as the Red Army's birthday. An emergency meeting held on 7 August 1927 put the blame for policy failure on Chen Duxiu, and replaced him as secretary-general with Qu Qiubai (1899–1935).

From September to November Mao led rural revolts in Hunan, known as the Autumn Harvest Uprising, but their failure led a meeting of the CCP Central Committee's provisional Politburo to dismiss him from his leadership positions within the CCP and its Hunan branch. This put Mao very much at odds both with the CCP central leadership and its Moscow backers. The end of the year saw another failed CCP-led armed uprising in Guangzhou, called the Guangzhou Commune, which cost the lives of several thousand workers and peasants. Meanwhile, in mid-November 1927 the peasant movement that Peng Pai had organized in southeastern Guangdong set up China's first ever soviet government in Lufeng, just east of Haifeng in Guangdong, but this and a similar one in Haifeng were both destroyed in March 1928, and Peng himself was executed in August 1929 near Shanghai. The CCP-led segments of the labour movement were also totally destroyed, as Chiang Kai-shek's labour policy lurched strongly to the right, with leftist trade unions suppressed and their leaders executed.

The issue of whether the CCP should seize cities or gradually expand its strength in the countryside reached its most intense point in 1930. In February the CCP's Central Committee issued a circular calling on the party to organize workers' strikes, local uprisings and army mutinies. It also asked the rurally based Red Army to try to take key cities and join in the workers' struggle. This was the line of Li Lisan (1889–1967), whose influence had dominated the CCP since the middle of 1929. Meanwhile Mao Zedong had established himself in the rural areas of Jiangxi Province, being joined by Zhu De and others in 1928. Mao and Zhu obeyed the February 1930 circular and in the summer CCP forces attempted to seize several major cities in the south, notably Changsha, the capital of Hunan, and its Jiangxi counterpart Nanchang. The CCP actually held Changsha briefly, but simply lacked the power to defend it and was inevitably driven out.

The retreat from Changsha convinced Mao of the futility of the Li Lisan line and, without Central Committee authorization, he decided to abandon all attempts to take large cities for the time being. According to Stuart Schram, 'the retreat from Changsha in September 1930 marked a crucial turning point in his thinking towards a relatively long-term strategy of encircling the cities from the countryside' (in Fairbank and Feuerwerker, 1986: 828). Moscow and the Comintern, which had been playing a highly ambiguous role in CCP affairs, turned against Li Lisan, forcing him from the CCP's leadership shortly after the Changsha fiasco.

In sum, by the end of 1930 the CCP had reached a very low ebb. Its leadership was in serious disarray. Its policies as an underground rebel group had chalked up many failures but few successes. Its main backers in Moscow did not understand its situation and could offer no effective advice or support (Rue, 1966).

THE CHINESE SOVIET REPUBLIC

Mao and his followers encountered both difficulties and successes in establishing red soviets in Jiangxi Province. By far the most important difficulty was the Futian Incident, which one of Mao's biographers has described as a 'loss of innocence' (Short, 1999: 265). In December 1930 in Futian, southern Jiangxi, soldiers Mao believed to be Li Lisan's supporters mutinied against him, setting up a soviet rival to his. Mao reacted with extreme brutality, not hesitating to have CCP comrades tortured in the most ghastly ways and killed if he doubted their loyalty. He took two months to suppress the mutiny, his forces killing over 2,000 people.

Despite this desperate power struggle, Mao succeeded in convening the week-long First All-China Soviet Congress in Ruijin, southeast Jiangxi. On its last day, 7 November 1931, the Congress proclaimed the **Chinese Soviet Republic**, with its capital in Ruijin, and adopted a constitution, a labour law and a land law. Having been expelled from coalition government in 1927, the CCP now formed its own state, often known simply as the Jiangxi Soviet, within the Chinese state.

The constitution announced the aim of overthrowing the rule of imperialism and the Nationalist Party (Brandt, Schwartz and Fairbank, 1971: 220–4). It declared that the Republic was 'a state based on the democratic dictatorship of the workers and peasants'. All power would 'belong to the workers, peasants, and Red Army soldiers and the entire toiling population'. Such groups would have the right to elect their own deputies to participate in government, but militarists, bureaucrats, landlords, gentry, village bosses and monks, as exploiting and counter-revolutionary elements, would be deprived of voting rights and of political freedom. The vital role of the

Chinese Soviet Republic: Also known as the Jiangxi Soviet, this was a state established in November 1931 with its capital in Ruijin, Jiangxi Province. It lasted until October 1934, when it was conquered by Nationalist Party troops.

masses, and the Marxist idea of class struggle, is strongly implied in such provisions. In addition, putting the workers first among the positive classes suggests that the CCP and its leader Mao were still convinced of the need for working-class leadership. One authority writes that during the whole period from the early 1920s to the mid-1940s, 'Mao continued to regard the industrial proletariat as the leading class of the Chinese Revolution', even while experience was forcing him to rely on the peasantry as its main force (Knight, 2007: 102).

One of the most striking features of the Chinese Soviet Republic was its radical land law (Brandt, Schwartz and Fairbank, 1971: 224–6). All big private landowners, including landlords, village bosses, gentry and militarists, were to be subject to confiscation of their land 'without any compensation whatever', whether or not they worked their own land or leased it out. Land would be distributed among the poor and middle peasants, with former owners not receiving any allotments. 'Hired farm hands, coolies, and toiling labourers shall enjoy equal rights to land allotments, irrespective of sex.'

In practice, this law was only partly successful. Despite the provisions of the constitution, some landowners found ways of retaining authority and even getting themselves into government. In 1933 Mao's regime carried out a land investigation, which aimed to increase production by promoting the enthusiasm of the masses and ferreting out hidden counter-revolutionaries. The results were not particularly impressive in economic terms and the movement lapsed. It resumed in the beginning of 1934. At this stage, 'the aims of the campaign were no longer principally economic . . . but political. It became a campaign against counter-revolutionaries, a red terror against landlords and rich peasants' (Jerome Ch'en, in Fairbank and Feuerwerker, 1986: 196).

Chiang Kai-shek carried out five 'encirclement campaigns' to destroy Mao's soviets. The first four ended in failure, but the fifth, which began towards the end of 1933, was more concentrated and much larger in scale. Chiang Kai-shek's strategy included building roads to increase his military mobility and blockading his enemy by moving peasants into villages that his troops could control. But the most important element was the building of a series of blockhouses that his troops could defend as others spread ever further into the red areas and towards Ruijin. By the autumn of 1934 Chiang Kai-shek's troops had succeeded in destroying the Chinese Soviet Republic. On 16 October Mao Zedong and Zhu De led their troops to the west, abandoning Ruijin and the central soviet area and beginning the famous Long March.

Plate 1 Three women in a cangue, a form of punishment in traditional China. This photograph was taken by an unknown photographer in 1907 in Shanghai.
Source: Corbis.

Plate 2 The main hall of the Wuchang Uprising Museum. This museum includes the hall where the first parliament of the revolution took place at the beginning of 1912, while Sun Yat-sen was still president.
Source: Colin Mackerras, December 1998.

Plate 3 Dr Sun Yat-sen 1866–1925.
First President of the Chinese Republic founded in 1912.
Source: Alamy.

Plate 4 Chiang Kai-shek (Jiang Jieshi), 1887–1975, Chinese statesman, in uniform.
Chiang was leader of the National Government from 1928 to 1949.
Source: Art Archive.

Plate 5 Mao Zedong, 1936. Shaanxi, China.
Source: Corbis.

Plate 6 Huaqing Pond outside Xi'an. Situated below Mount Li (in the background), this is the place where Chiang Kai-shek was staying when he was kidnapped in December 1936.
Source: Colin Mackerras, May 2007.

Plate 7 Chiang Kai-shek's desk in the compound Huaqing Pond, exactly as it was when he was kidnapped in December 1936.
Source: Colin Mackerras, May 2007.

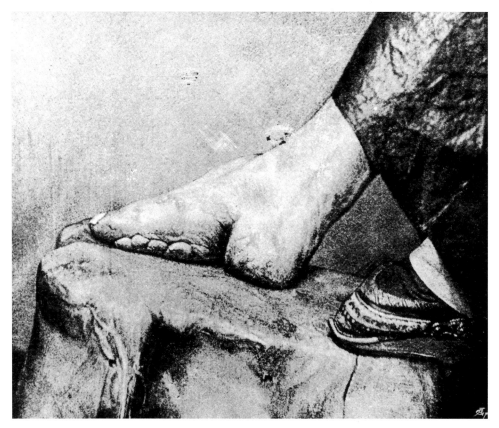

Plate 8 A close-up of the feet of an aristocratic Chinese woman, deformed by binding. Foot binding in China was condemned by the government in 1902.
Source: Original publication: *Illustrated London News* – pub. 14 July 1900. Getty Images.

Plate 9 The prayer hall of the great Yutian Mosque. The architectural style is typical of the mosques of the Turkic Islamic peoples of Xinjiang.
Source: Colin Mackerras, October 2003.

Plate 10 Mei Lanfang in the drama 'Unofficial History of the Imperial Concubine'
(Taizhen waishi), premiered in 1926. Mei plays the role of Yang Yuhuan
(died 756), a historical figure and the favourite concubine of Emperor Xuanzong
(reigned 712–56).
Source: Mei Lanfang Memorial Museum.

THE LONG MARCH

Mao Zedong claimed that the significance of the Long March lay in the fact that it was 'the first of its kind in the annals of history' **[Doc. 24, p. 135]**. Speaking just after its completion, Mao could well be forgiven this high evaluation of its achievement. Dick Wilson's authoritative account largely agrees, and he begins by summing it up as 'the most extraordinary march in human history' (Wilson, 1971: xiii). It is true that several later accounts have been somewhat more critical of the CCP leadership's role in the Long March. In particular, Sun (2006: 179) portrays Mao, 'the sophisticated and ruthless politician', as more interested in power than ideology or the people's welfare. She is extremely critical of the human cost of the Long March, especially for the women who took part, and the lack of reward they received from the CCP when it got to government. However, her study of surviving Long Marchers left her still deeply inspired by their 'courage, their idealism, optimism and faith' (Sun, 2006: 279).

What happened was that, instead of giving up in the face of the destruction of their Republic, Mao and his Red Army undertook a march of some 12,000 kilometres to take them in an enormous arc to northern Shaanxi Province. They traversed some extraordinarily difficult terrain, including swamplands and mountains, and crossed over some two dozen rivers. All the time, they were pursued by Nationalist Party and provincial warlord troops and fought numerous skirmishes, spending over two weeks in major battles. They suffered horrendous casualties, with only some 5–10 per cent of those 100,000 or so who had begun surviving the full length of the march, though it is only fair to add that some remained behind as guerrillas and others joined along the way. Because they treated local communities with a respect matched neither by the warlord nor Nationalist Party troops, their reception was generally very positive. There were exceptions to this pattern, for instance in a Tibetan area one queen was so hostile to Chinese of any kind that she threatened to boil alive anybody who helped the Red Army (Wilson, 1971: 221). But the fact remains that, seriously defeated in Jiangxi, the Red Army succeeded in escaping to a new set of bases in northern Shaanxi, and went on to gain power over the whole country. This would not have been possible without the Long March and signifies an achievement of enormous proportions, though it needs to be added that this verdict does not deny the gigantic cost to Mao's followers and others in terms of suffering.

Even during the Long March, serious struggles for power persisted within the CCP. At a major conference in Zunyi, Guizhou Province, held from 6 to 8 January 1935, Mao Zedong attacked the policies that had led to the fall of the Chinese Soviet Republic, thus laying the blame on others for the disaster that had befallen the party. His views won the support of such major figures as Zhou Enlai and Zhu De, and the upshot of the Zunyi Conference was 'his emergence as the most influential CCP leader'. However, Mao's near total dominance of the CCP still lay a few years in the future, and it was not until 1943 that his triumph became 'irreversible' (Teiwes with Sun, 1994: 65).

Another power struggle took place in the summer of 1935 during a meeting between two major groupings within the Red Army, those of Mao and Zhang Guotao, in northwestern Sichuan Province. Mao was determined to go north, since it was there he could best resist Japan. Zhang disagreed with this strategy, with the result that the two split up. In the meantime, however, on 1 August 1935, the CCP had issued a document called 'Appeal to Fellow-countrymen to Resist Japan and for National Salvation', advocating a united-front policy with Chiang Kai-shek against the Japanese. The CCP was thus at the forefront of resistance to Japan, winning it much political support. Chiang was still following a policy of conciliation towards the Japanese at the time, and hostility to Japanese advances was a major issue for Chinese nationalism.

THE YAN'AN DECADE

In October 1935 Mao's forces arrived in northern Shaanxi, and the Long March was over. In December 1936 they moved their headquarters to the small town of Yan'an, retaining control there until evicted by Chiang Kai-shek's troops in March 1947. Over these years, Mao and his supporters developed a model that Mark Selden (1971) has dubbed 'the Yan'an way in revolutionary China'.

Mao followed two tightly related policies during most of the years of the Yan'an decade. The first was resistance to Japan. Territory under CCP control expanded steadily behind Japanese lines and despite constant Japanese attacks. Many patriotic intellectuals went from the cities to Yan'an, believing it to be the main focus of the anti-Japanese struggle. When the War Against Japan broke out in 1937 (see next chapter), there were only about 40,000 CCP members, but in his report to the Seventh Congress in April 1945, Mao (1965: III, 317) estimated membership at over 1.2 million. One important school of thought (Johnson, 1962) even lists the growth of peasant nationalism, resulting from the struggle against Japan, as the most important reason why the CCP was able to win against the Nationalist Party in 1949.

The other prong of Mao's policy was social revolution. Although this policy was radical by the standards of the Nationalist Party or Japanese, it is worth noting that it was a retreat on the Jiangxi Soviet. In the interests of the united front, the CCP adopted a land policy of rent and interest reduction, not confiscation, which was generally restricted to those cases where rich families had gone off to Japanese-controlled cities or collaborated with the Japanese. Although tax policy was designed to favour the poor against the rich, it did not usually involve confiscation of property.

Mao and his followers also educated the peasants to take an interest in government. The chief organs of power at district and regional levels were elected people's councils, with all adult villagers having the vote, no matter what their class. The CCP also got the peasants to form numerous mass associations, such as for women or young people, and these enjoyed some say in local government.

Economic policy rested on the principle of self-reliance, made necessary by enemy blockades. Since this was a very poor region, the government encouraged the voluntary formation of mutual aid teams and cooperatives, remuneration being based on contribution in terms of labour and investment, such as tools, land and animals. It also set up some low-level industry, creating the beginnings of a working class.

Although the CCP's achievements in the Yan'an region should not be underestimated, there was a sharp edge to Mao's rule there. The CCP was run along Leninist lines with a strict hierarchy and lines of control **[Doc. 25, p. 136]**. At the same time, Mao insisted on a very significant role for the masses in the revolution. Maintaining the balance between the party and the masses thus became very difficult indeed, with CCP members frequently unclear at which point leadership turned into commandism.

In the early 1940s Mao carried out his **Rectification Movement** in the various CCP-controlled areas throughout the country with the aim of imposing his version of Marxist-Leninist orthodoxy on the party. In theory the deviant should not be punished but persuaded towards the 'correct' line. But as one writer aptly notes, 'intense small-group discussions, criticism and self-criticism, the demand for repeatedly rewritten confessions of error, and at the extreme the use of brainwashing – the destruction of the personality of the "patient" by a combination of psychological pressure and physical deprivation – all these techniques first came into general use in the Rectification Movement' (Gray, 1990: 283). And it hardly needs emphasis that they frequently caused the most extreme anguish to CCP members unwilling to toe the line.

> **Rectification Movement:** A campaign orchestrated by Mao Zedong in the early 1940s in Yan'an and surrounding CCP-controlled areas aimed at imposing his own authority and his brand of Marxism-Leninism on the CCP.

Moreover, one biography of Mao dismisses the early 1940s in Yan'an as nothing more or less than a terror, with Mao's activities all aimed not at social revolution but only at building his own power, including a strong personality cult. 'People who lived through this period all remembered it as a turning point when they "firmly established in our minds that Chairman Mao is our only wise leader"'. As for the CCP's Seventh Congress of April 1945, Mao's personality cult simply signalled that he 'had become the Stalin of the CCP' (Chang and Halliday, 2005: 278, 279).

9

The War Against Japan

At the end of 1936 Chiang Kai-shek was belatedly forced to give top priority to fighting the Japanese. About six months later came the outbreak of the War Against Japan, or Second Sino-Japanese War, which the Chinese usually know as the War of Resistance Against Japan. Lasting until 1945, the war became enmeshed with the Second World War. James Sheridan (1975: 245) rightly describes the decade following 1937 as one 'of death and destruction'. The war was also extremely important in Chinese history, with implications likely to remain for a long time to come **[Doc. 26, p. 136]**.

THE XI'AN INCIDENT AND THE SECOND UNITED FRONT

A crisis flared in China at the end of 1936, shaking all China and Chiang Kai-shek, then at the height of his popularity. At the beginning of December, Chiang had gone to Xi'an, capital of Shaanxi Province, to coordinate a final attack on the CCP, which he thought much reduced in force following the Long March. The attacking army, the Northwest Bandit-Suppression Force, consisted mostly of soldiers from Manchuria and was to be led by Zhang Xueliang, the Manchurian warlord and son of Zhang Zuolin, often called the Young Marshal. Zhang Xueliang was not enthusiastic about the campaign, because he and his troops were convinced that the real enemy was not the CCP, but the Japanese.

On 12 December Zhang took the extreme step of placing Chiang Kai-shek under house arrest, demanding that he promise to give up the war against the CCP, and instead fight the Japanese. Some of Zhang's followers even advocated killing Chiang, but Zhang himself resolutely rejected this course.

The CCP leaders in northern Shaanxi were heavily involved in the **Xi'an Incident** and had been informed of Zhang's plan to kidnap Chiang. They took part in the negotiations over Chiang's release and Zhou Enlai flew to Xi'an on 15 December. The CCP and Young Marshal had a common interest in fighting Japan. Almost certainly Mao saw the likelihood of a great increase in his own power if Chiang were kept in prison and humiliated and may even have thought that, with Chiang out of the way, he might seize power himself. When Stalin cabled ordering Chiang's release, Mao flew into a rage and initially ignored the instruction.

On 25 December Chiang was released, returning to Nanjing together with his erstwhile captor, whom he shortly had court-martialled and imprisoned. Although he signed no formal agreements, Chiang had come to realize the necessity of giving top priority to fighting Japan. Chiang never forgave Zhang Xueliang and even took him as a prisoner to Taiwan when defeated in 1949. On the other hand, after lengthy negotiations that were hastened, no doubt, by the outbreak of the war, Chiang and the CCP did form their second united front. They agreed to abandon the fight against each other, at least for the time being. In particular, the Communists agreed to absorb their own troops into China's and on 22 August 1937 the Red Army formally became the Chinese national army's Eighth Route Army. As one scholar puts it (Terrill, 1995: 169), Chiang 'had given up the pretense of unique governmental authority in China' as a result of the Xi'an Incident. Mao may not have been able to seize power at this stage, but he had done pretty well from the incident. Chang and Halliday (2005: 196) comment that the main effect for the CCP was that this small party 'had just been promoted to a major "opposition party"'.

Xi'an Incident: The kidnap of Chiang Kai-shek in December 1936 to force him to resist Japan.

THE WAR AGAINST JAPAN: EARLY STAGES, 1937–40

The date when historians mark the beginning of the War Against Japan is 7 July 1937. What happened on that day was that Japanese troops attacked a town just south of the Lugou Bridge (also called Marco Polo Bridge in the West), itself just outside Beiping (as it was then called, now Beijing). It is not absolutely clear that the Japanese intended the outbreak of war through this action, but certainly they had seized both Beiping and nearby Tianjin by the end of the month.

In August 1937 the Japanese began a second front, attacking and seizing Shanghai in the south. From September Japanese planes bombed the Chinese capital Nanjing, forcing Chiang Kai-shek to abandon the city for

Wuhan. Japanese troops, under General Iwane Matsui, completed their occupation of Nanjing on 13 December. They then began what has gone down in history as the Nanjing Massacre or 'Rape of Nanjing' and among the most atrocious massacres in modern history **[Doc. 27, p. 137]**. In an orgy of slaughter and rape, which spared neither the very old nor small children, neither little girls nor ancient women, the Japanese troops went berserk, killing at least 100,000 people and possibly as many as over 300,000 over an extended period of several weeks. (For the lower number see Doc. 27 and for the higher Lin Wusun in Xu, 1995: 7.) It is possible that Matsui himself was not actually the main culprit. Edward Behr (1987: 240) claims that he was a devout Buddhist and that his orders were 'exemplary': the troops were to enter in an orderly fashion with the aim of persuading the Chinese to 'place their confidence in Japan'. In the event, however, it was Matsui whom the International Military Tribunal of the Far East held as mainly responsible for the massacre, sentencing him to death **[Doc. 28, p. 137]**.

The effect of the Nanjing Massacre was the opposite of what Matsui intended: it galvanized the Chinese to more intense resistance. However, despite the vigour with which Chiang Kai-shek carried on the fight, Chinese troops were not particularly effective. One episode in the war's early stages serves as an example. The Japanese tried to seize Taierzhuang in southern Shandong as a gateway to taking the major city of Xuzhou in far north-western Jiangsu. The Battle of Taierzhuang saw bitter fighting from late March 1938, with the Chinese claiming victory on 7 April, inflicting very heavy casualties on the Japanese. This did not, however, prevent the Japanese from taking Xuzhou soon after anyway.

In June 1938 Nationalist Party troops burst the dykes of the Yellow River near Zhengzhou, Henan Province, to prevent the southward advance of the Japanese armies. The effect was to cause devastating flooding in many places, with many people drowned and enormous losses to crops, property and houses. Perhaps even more dramatic was that the Yellow River actually changed its course to empty itself into the Huai River, with the result that it flowed into the sea a long way south of its earlier mouth in Shandong.

The flooding of the Yellow River stalled the Japanese for three months. They then resumed their advance and attacked Wuhan in south-central China, taking it with much devastation and extremely heavy casualties in October 1938. Chiang Kai-shek fled to Chongqing in inland Sichuan Province, which became his wartime capital.

With their military dominance apparent in China, the Japanese launched a political initiative that they hoped would lead to China's surrender. On 3 November 1938 the Japanese prime minister Prince Konoe Fumimaro issued a statement on the 'new order in East Asia' with six principles, including permanent stability for East Asia, joint defence against communism, economic cooperation and world peace. Although phrased in high-sounding terms, this was actually a manifesto for the domination of China.

The senior members of the Nationalist Party were not at one over how to react. Some, including Wang Jingwei, were alarmed by China's failures against Japan and believed there was hope for peace in accepting Japan's terms. Wang flew to Hanoi, where he began a 'peace movement'. On 22 December Konoe announced that he would destroy the National Government, establishing a new one that would be friendly to Japan. Chiang Kai-shek denounced the plan as aimed at the 'annexation and total extinction' of China.

In June 1939 Wang Jingwei went to Tokyo to discuss the formation of a Japanese-sponsored regime in China. Despite Chiang's order for his arrest, Wang Jingwei established himself in March 1940 as the formal head of the Japanese-sponsored National Government of the Republic of China, with its capital in Nanjing. The Axis powers and their allies recognized his regime, but most countries continued their support for Chiang Kai-shek's government.

Why a man who had ranked so high in the Nationalist Party and been so sympathetic to the left should take this action remains unclear. Immanuel Hsü (1995: 586) has suggested four reasons, including pessimism and defeatism over China's prospects for winning the war, hatred and rivalry towards Chiang Kai-shek, and concern for the welfare of the people in the Japanese-occupied areas. These are perhaps charitable explanations. In his last testament to his country, which was actually published in Hong Kong in 1964, Wang himself offered a reason rather similar to the one about concern for the welfare of people in the Japanese-occupied areas. He said (quoted Boyle, 1972: 351–2):

> The reason that I sullied my good name and disregarded my glorious past record of dedicating myself to state affairs for forty years was because at a time of national emergency, we cannot preserve the life of our state unless we depend upon our wits. If we can take advantage of the enemy's lack of caution and restore territory and console the homeless people – if I could do that – I don't care how difficult the remainder of my life might be.

It is now clear that Wang Jingwei's policy and actions were a disastrous failure. Not only did he become more and more alienated from the prevailing mood of his country, but he was never able to restore territory or console the homeless people through his actions. It is hardly surprising that the situation for Wang's regime became even more desperate after Pearl Harbor. According to Boyle (1972: 349) the US entry into the war 'broke the spirit' of many of Wang's supporters 'and gave rise to a live-for-today outlook on life'. Wang Jingwei died in Japan in November 1944 of illnesses and infections resulting from an assassination attempt against him in 1935.

Despite the achievements of his early career, Wang Jingwei has suffered excoriation as a collaborator by virtually all factions of Chinese politics. Although his death spared him the ignominy of a postwar trial, his senior followers were shot as traitors shortly after war's end.

THE WAR AGAINST JAPAN: LATER STAGES, 1941–5

Although the united front with the CCP lasted throughout the war, there was frequent conflict between the Nationalist and Communist Parties, including military clashes. One of particular importance was the Southern Anhui Incident of January 1941. There is disagreement over who was to blame, but what happened was that Nationalist Party troops killed or captured a large contingent of the CCP's New Fourth Army in southern Anhui. The CCP reacted by accusing Chiang Kai-shek of wishing to resume civil war. However, Lyman Van Slyke (in Eastman et al., 1991: 329) claims that the incident ended not the united front but the worst conflict between the two parties. His view is that in most places 'the balance of power among Chinese forces behind Japanese lines had come by mid-1941 to favour the CCP' and that struggle was political after that, not military.

By the end of 1941 Chiang Kai-shek was in a much weakened position in relation both to the CCP and the Japanese. Yet he was hardly on the point of surrender, as shown by the success of his troops in resisting a major Japanese attempt to seize the Hunan capital Changsha. As one authority notes (Ch'i in Hsiung and Levine, 1992: 157), 'for fifty-three long months, beginning in July 1937, China stood alone, single-handedly fighting an undeclared war against Japan'. It is hardly surprising that Chiang and the Chinese in general were delighted when the USA was forced into the war against Japan through the latter's attack on Pearl Harbor in December, since it altered the balance of forces and changed the nature of the war decisively in their favour.

In the first place, the USA immediately became closely involved in the war in China. The Allies established the China-Burma-India theatre of war, with Chiang Kai-shek accepting as supreme command of the China theatre at the beginning of 1942. In March US General Joseph Stilwell took up command as Chiang Kai-shek's chief-of-staff in the Chinese theatre, signalling a great increase in American military power in China.

Although the Western powers had begun giving China financial aid before 1941, the Soviet Union had been somewhat more generous, but Pearl Harbor changed the situation drastically. In February 1942 President Roosevelt approved a credit loan of US$500 million in aid to China, by far the largest in a series from the USA and Britain to that time. Already inflation was becoming a serious problem for the Chinese currency, and early in 1942 Chiang's government set up a Price Stabilization Fund, to which the USA contributed very significantly.

In addition, China made considerable progress diplomatically in its relations with the West. During the Nanjing decade China had tried to win revision of the unequal treaties it had signed with the powers during the nineteenth and early twentieth centuries. There were achievements but, according to Edmund Fung (in Pong and Fung, 1985: 185), the performance of Chiang's government in foreign relations 'was a failure on the whole', being based on 'the diplomacy of weakness'. However, a new situation emerged with the War Against Japan. On 11 January 1943 China signed new treaties in Chongqing with both the USA and Britain. Both treaties provided for:

- the abolition of extraterritoriality (see Chapter 2);
- the handing over of all Concessions to the National Government, Britain retaining only Hong Kong;
- the abrogation of the Boxer Protocol (see Chapter 3).

China later signed similar treaties with a range of other countries. Moreover, Chiang Kai-shek's personal standing rose greatly when, together with US President Roosevelt and British Prime Minister Winston Churchill, he attended the important Cairo Conference in November 1943. The Cairo Declaration (1 December) stated that Manchuria and Taiwan would revert to China after the victory.

These positive developments should not hide continuing disasters, both domestically and in foreign relations. In 1942 and 1943 there took place what White and Jacoby (1946: 176) call 'the greatest disaster of the war in China', namely a major drought-famine **[Doc. 29, p. 138]**. Centred on Henan Province, where it killed probably well over 2 million people, this catastrophe affected several other provinces, including Shaanxi, Hubei, Shandong and Sichuan. Along with taxation exactions, this famine led on to a peasant revolt that saw Chinese turning against their own troops and allowing the Japanese to 'cut through the Chinese lines the way a butcher knife cuts through butter' (White and Jacoby, 1946: 178). There were Chinese traitors and collaborators aplenty, but 'never before had the unorganized peasants turned in cold blood against their national troops while they were fighting the enemy' (White and Jacoby, 1946: 179).

Meanwhile, the relations of the Chinese government with the powers were not entirely smooth. In particular, Chiang Kai-shek and Joseph Stilwell, to put it mildly, did not get on with each other. Stilwell, who was so hot-tempered by personality as to earn the nickname Vinegar Joe, referred to Chiang contemptuously as 'the peanut', believing him still too unwilling to work cooperatively with the CCP against Japan. In September 1944 matters came to a head when Stilwell had a major fight with Chiang, quoting Roosevelt as planning to give him (Stilwell) unrestricted command of the Chinese forces. Chiang Kai-shek could not possibly accept such a verdict about his own troops in his own country. Brigadier-General Patrick Hurley, whom Roosevelt had sent to China in August to try and settle relations between Chiang and Stilwell, advised Roosevelt that he must dismiss Stilwell or risk losing Chiang and, with him, China. In October 1944 Roosevelt replaced Stilwell with the mild-mannered and conciliatory Albert Wedemeyer.

Meanwhile in July the first batch of the US Military Observers (DIXIE) Mission had arrived in Yan'an to evaluate the potential for anti-Japanese military collaboration with the CCP, the Mission reporting very enthusiastically about the CCP and their future role in China. In November Hurley and Mao Zedong even signed an agreement in Yan'an by which the CCP reaffirmed its intention to work for Japan's defeat by obeying a coalition National Government.

The background to these 1944 developments in military terms was Japan's most significant offensive since 1938, the Transcontinental Offensive or *Ichigo* (literally 'Operation Number One'). Lasting from April to November 1944, this vast offensive seized large tracts of Chinese territory from north to south, captured the previously impregnable city of Changsha, and for the first time established control over railways linking Korea with Vietnam. Although the Japanese made no attempt to seize Chongqing, this offensive was a gigantic defeat for the Nationalists who bore the brunt of the fighting, inflicting nearly 500,000 casualties on their armies and enormous losses in government finances (Boyle, 1972; Ch'i, 1982; Eastman, 1984). The fact that the Japanese advance took place so near the end of the war suggests strongly that China's eventual victory was due mainly to the Americans and their overall triumph in the Pacific War, with Chiang Kai-shek's government deserving only little of the credit.

10

Postwar China, the Civil War

A t the end of the War Against Japan in 1945, Chiang Kai-shek was strong internationally and the odds appeared greatly in his favour domestically **[Doc. 30, p. 139]**. Yet the war had weakened him greatly, while the CCP was much stronger at the end of the war than at the beginning. Hardly had victory against Japan restored peace in 1945 than China faced yet another war, the Civil War between Chiang Kai-shek and the Chinese Communist Party (CCP). Lasting from 1946 till 1949, this resulted in a victory for the CCP, which established the People's Republic of China on 1 October 1949.

BETWEEN WARS: FROM THE VICTORY OVER JAPAN TO THE OUTBREAK OF CIVIL WAR

Chiang's international strength at the end of the War Against Japan was much stronger than at the beginning. By far the most important sign of this rise was that, when the United Nations Organization was formed in May–June 1945, China held a permanent seat on the Security Council, being thus promoted to be among the five greatest powers of the age. This decision was taken at American insistence and was, for example, initially opposed by British Prime Minister Winston Churchill, who considered it 'a piece of tomfoolery' (McAleavy, 1967: 316). Since that time, there have been many challenges concerning China's role in the United Nations, but nobody has seriously contested its right to be ranked among the permanent five members of the Security Council.

In contrast to his standing internationally, Chiang's domestic position at war's end was weaker than it had been at the time of Japan's invasion. China had taken enormous military casualties, officially 1,319,958 killed, with incalculable civilian casualties. China's economy had all but collapsed. Apart from the destruction wreaked by warfare, the great inflation of 1937–49, among the most severe examples of this ailment in all history, had already reached extremely serious proportions.

Chiang Kai-shek's government lacked the administrative structure to take over the country effectively after the Japanese defeat. It had also become thoroughly corrupt. Both the military and civilian officials involved in the takeover of the country 'scrambled to appropriate for their own use property owned or occupied by the Japanese and their collaborators' (Pepper, 1978: 424). Workers could not deal with the period of unemployment brought about by the suspension of industrial production in the recovered areas, with the result that the long dormant labour movement revived. Industrialists who had sustained the economy in the interior during the war found themselves facing bankruptcy when promised government compensation failed to materialize.

Meanwhile, the CCP had actually done quite well from the war. Its Seventh Congress, held in Yan'an from April to June 1945, announced the population of its liberated areas as 95.5 million. Mao was very clear that the CCP should share in the fruits of victory in the form of participation in a coalition government.

At the end of August 1945, a few days before Japan's formal surrender, US Ambassador Patrick Hurley accompanied Mao Zedong and Zhou Enlai from Yan'an for negotiations over a coalition government. Their destination was Chongqing, which remained Chiang's capital until moved back to Nanjing in May 1946. Although the Chongqing negotiations yielded a joint resolution to avoid civil war and build an independent, free and strong new China, many questions remained unresolved and the National Government refused to recognize the CCP's liberated areas. A committee was established to consider the absorption of both parties' troops into a single national army. For Mao himself the Chongqing negotiations were beneficial, because he talked to Chiang Kai-shek as an equal, and 'Foreign embassies invited him not as a rebel, but as a statesman' (Chang and Halliday, 2005: 297). In essence, however, the negotiations did not get far.

Meanwhile, the Soviet Union was becoming heavily involved in the northeastern region of China. As noted in Chapter 9, the Cairo Declaration of December 1943 had stated that the then Japanese-occupied Manchuria (Manchukoku) would revert to China after the victory. The Soviet Union had signed a neutrality pact with Japan in 1941, but in the last days of the war Soviet troops entered Manchuria. On 14 August 1945, the same day that the Japanese Emperor issued his order for unconditional surrender, Chiang Kai-shek's government signed a Treaty of Friendship and Alliance with the Soviet

Union in Moscow. The Soviet Union recognized Chiang Kai-shek as the leader of China, and promised not to support his enemies. Soviet troops would shortly withdraw from Manchuria. In return, Chiang Kai-shek made several major concessions in Manchuria, including partially handing over the two main railways there to the Soviet Union and granting the right to station troops in the ports then called Port Arthur (Lüshun) and Dairen (Dalian, both in Liaoning Province) and surrounding areas. In addition, the treaty in effect gave independence to what Chiang knew as Outer Mongolia, an eventuality he had fiercely resisted to that time, and continued to oppose after being forced to retreat to Taiwan.

Soviet troops began withdrawing from Manchuria in March 1946. There is significant disagreement on who benefited. Suzanne Pepper (1978: 213) claims that from mid-August to mid-November 1945 Soviet troops occupied the cities and major lines of communication, while 'CCP forces entered Manchuria with the acquiescence if not the active cooperation of the Soviet occupation forces'. She adds that she doubts the Soviet troops 'could have prevented this penetration even had they tried, which they apparently did not'. On the other hand, John Melby (1969: 25) claims the CCP expected the Soviets to welcome them in Manchuria. While the Soviets had promised not to support Chiang Kai-shek's enemies the CCP, they were, after all, ideologically aligned. 'They were dismayed when the Russians not only denied them military help, but excluded them as far as possible'. There is agreement that the CCP took control of the countryside anyway, a fact that was to be of enormous importance for their victory later on.

In November 1945, when it had become obvious that the Chongqing negotiations had yielded nothing worthwhile or permanent, Hurley resigned as ambassador over the failure of US China policy. US President Harry Truman sent George C. Marshall as special envoy with the rank of ambassador to succeed him. Discussions continued and in January 1946 he, Zhang Qun for the Nationalists and Zhou Enlai for the CCP even signed a ceasefire and agreed to convoke a Political Consultative Conference, which actually sat until the end of the month. However, though the Conference agreed to nationalize the army in principle, it soon became clear that what both sides wanted was victory, not compromise. After continuing negotiations, the ceasefire finally collapsed in the middle of 1946 and full-scale civil war erupted. Although the Marshall mission did not actually end until early the following year, it was already obvious that Marshall, like Hurley, had failed to mediate peace.

THE CIVIL WAR AND THE VICTORY OF THE CCP

With the outbreak of civil war, Chiang Kai-shek's troops launched several offensives and at first appeared to do very well. In the second half of 1946 he won a string a victories, capturing 165 towns and 174,000 square kilometres. On 19 March 1947 he even took the CCP capital Yan'an. Although Chiang Kai-shek thought this action was final, he was shortly to be disappointed because by the middle of the year the **People's Liberation Army** (PLA), the new name for the CCP's troops, had launched several large and successful counter-offensives, which in effect had turned the tide against the Nationalists. On 10 October 1947 the PLA issued a manifesto calling for a united front of 'workers, peasants, soldiers, intellectuals and businessmen, all oppressed classes, all people's organizations, democratic parties, minority nationalities, overseas Chinese and other patriots' to overthrow Chiang Kai-shek (Mackerras, 1982: 426). By the middle of 1948, the number of Nationalist Party troops, which had stood at some 3.7 million at the end of the war in August 1945, had fallen to 2.2 million, and those that remained were extremely demoralized and even disloyal **[Doc. 31, p. 140]**. On the other hand, the CCP's troops, only 320,000 in August 1945, had risen to 1.5 million in number.

People's Liberation Army: *Renmin jiefang jun,* the name given to the CCP's forces from 1 May 1946.

The Political Consultative Conference of January 1946 had declared that a reorganized government would end the period of tutelage and formally adopt the revised draft of the 1936 constitution (see Chapter 7). In November 1946 Chiang Kai-shek convoked a National Constitutional Assembly which next month formally adopted the 1936 revised constitution. A highly liberal document, this constitution laid down universal suffrage and elections, secret ballot and equality for all people.

However, the constitution was not due to go into effect for a year, so as to give time for government reorganization. This process proved very difficult, especially since the CCP had made clear that it had no intention of participating, even though a few government positions were reserved for its leaders. After all, since the middle of 1946 the country had been in a state of civil war and the CCP believed more and more firmly that they could win total power. On his side, Chiang Kai-shek was ever more fearful for the preservation of his power, and was becoming more and more repressive. By the time the constitution came into operation, time had run out for Chiang Kai-shek.

Meanwhile two related trends exacerbated Chiang Kai-shek's problems. Neither was new in the immediate aftermath of the War Against Japan, but both got considerably worse when civil war erupted in mid-1946. One was the labour movement, the other economic decline symbolized above all by an acceleration of inflation.

Chiang Kai-shek's response to the strikes that broke out after the end of the War Against Japan was a kind of carrot and stick approach. His policy was to attempt to peg wages against the cost of living but also take over the labour movement so that his government could control it and keep it in order. On 24 April 1946 the Executive Yuan ordered that all labour disputes must come before government arbitration. He moved against the independent Chinese Labour Association (CLA) on the grounds that it was necessary to control Communist agitators bent on exploiting labour unrest. In August 1946 armed police took over the Chongqing office of the CLA, an action followed by others of a similar kind. At the same time, the government set up many of its own trade unions.

While it is true that the number of strikes fell to a low point in June 1946, this success proved illusory and temporary. A recession in the second half of 1946 threw many people out of work. By the end of 1946 one estimate put the number of unemployed in the capital Nanjing at about 200,000, or about 30 per cent of the total population. December 1946 saw strikes escalating, the number in Shanghai being more than in any other month since the victory against Japan, with the government powerless to take preventative action (Pepper, 1978: 109). And this was but a prelude to a much worse situation that was to follow, as strikes, work slowdowns and protests multiplied in number and seriousness. As for the issue of pegging wages against the cost of living, this turned into a black joke because of the speed in the rise of prices of necessary commodities.

In January 1947 inflation shot up to unprecedented heights, while speculation on the currency only made matters worse, with rates increasingly spiralling out of control. The government made several attempts to stabilize the economy, most notably in August 1948 when it inaugurated a new currency, fixed an exchange rate with the old currency and banned strikes and demonstrations. These attempts failed dismally. One example will suffice to show the seriousness of the problem. On 20 September 1948 a group at the University of Nanjing announced that it had measured the wholesale price index for Nanjing at 8,740,600, as compared with 1,335,303 in June 1948 and 5,485 in August 1946 (see Mackerras, 1982: 431), and inflation continued to accelerate in the following months.

One of Chiang Kai-shek's main responses to this economic deterioration was to appeal for more and more aid from the USA. Chiang thought he could rely on the Americans, because the rivalry between the USA and the Soviet Union would make the former desperate not to lose China to communism. In the 1948 American elections, the Republican presidential candidate

Thomas Dewey promised massive financial and military aid to Chiang Kai-shek if he won the elections, but to worldwide surprise he lost them to Democrat Harry S. Truman, who in November and December 1948 rejected Chiang's pleas for further assistance.

American aid may have been important, though whether it was crucial is not so certain. What is quite clear, however, is that the cumulative effects of various trends, including a series of student movements (see Chapter 12), together with the political, economic and foreign policy issues discussed in the preceding paragraphs, produced a disastrous effect on the morale of the people. By the end of 1948 it was a very common conviction among Chinese that nothing could be worse than a continuation of the Nationalist Party regime. A piece written at the end of 1948 by distinguished commentator A. Doak Barnett found that almost everybody in the southern provinces of Jiangsu, Zhejiang, Jiangxi, Hunan and Guangdong were 'psychologically prepared for a basic shift of political control and a change of regime' **[Doc. 32, p. 140]**.

It was against this background that the final acts of what the CCP calls the War of Liberation took place. The first major result of the offensive that began in October 1947 was in Manchuria or the northeast. By the middle of March 1948, PLA troops commanded by Lin Biao had seized the whole of the northeast, apart from a few major cities. On 2 November 1948 the CCP capture of Shenyang signalled the complete loss of the northeast to Chiang Kai-shek's government.

The PLA moved towards the south and formed a pincer against the major cities of Tianjin and Beiping. The Nationalist Party defender, General Fu Zuoyi, who had earlier inflicted defeats on the CCP, had a large resistance force, but is said to have lost his defence plans due to a Communist agent operating in his headquarters (Hsü, 1995: 632). Tianjin fell on 15 January 1949 after a sharp fight. As for Beiping, Fu Zuoyi decided to surrender the city without a battle, which he feared would spell destruction, or at least damage, to the priceless old buildings and artefacts there, and it fell on 31 January 1949.

Further south, PLA troops under Marshall Chen Yi had seized Shandong Province and on 6 November 1948 launched what was to become the historic Huaihai Campaign. With hundreds of thousands of troops deployed on both sides, the PLA victory in this battle in January 1949 opened the way towards Chiang Kai-shek's capital Nanjing on the lower reaches of the Yangzi River. With Nanjing's fall on 23 April 1949, the PLA met comparatively little resistance in the south.

Chiang Kai-shek went back to Chongqing in August, planning a last stand in the southwest. However, the PLA took the city at the end of November, and Chiang Kai-shek fled to nearby Chengdu, Sichuan Province. This was his point of departure when he flew from the Chinese mainland for the last time on 10 December 1949, bound for Taibei. (See also Chassin, 1965; Eastman, 1984; Pepper, 1978.)

Meanwhile, in Beiping the CCP organized their own Chinese People's Political Consultative Conference, consisting of various political forces hostile to Chiang Kai-shek and his Nationalist Party. It was this body which, in September 1949, declared the city again the Chinese capital, changing its name back to Beijing, and adopted a provisional constitution known as the Common Programme. On 1 October 1949 Mao Zedong held a large rally in the centre of Beijing, at which he declared the establishment of a new regime: the People's Republic of China.

Part 3

THEMES OF CHANGE

11

Aspects of Social Change: Family and Women, Religion and Secular Ideology

The first half of the twentieth century was a period of considerable but uneven social change. Two dichotomies are particularly evident. One is that between persistent traditions and the influence of modern ideas, mostly coming from the West and the Soviet Union. The other is that between the city and the countryside. It was the cities where foreign influences were most powerful and where change took hold most strongly. Change occurred in the countryside too, and nationalist ideas percolated there in various ways, such as through village schools. But change was stifled by the imperatives of survival and the drudgery of unmechanized farming.

FAMILY LIFE

A patriarchal and hierarchical family system stood at the heart of traditional Confucianism. Since ancestor worship was among the most important of all practices, at least among the elite, the production of a male heir was crucial. Marriage was more a partnership between two families than between two individuals, and the prevailing practice was for parents to arrange spouses for their children with the aid of matchmakers. As a result, romantic love was not a prerequisite for a marriage partner, and it was not necessary for a man even to meet his wife before the wedding day, let alone know her well. Divorce was available to men on a range of grounds, but not to women. Rich men could keep concubines in addition to a main wife, but absolute fidelity was demanded of women, even when widowed.

The May Fourth Movement was bitterly opposed to the traditional family system, believing it oppressive and against the interests of young people, especially women. It was, in particular, hostile to the notion of arranged marriages, and proponents propagated freedom in the choice of spouses loudly and fervently **[Doc. 33, p. 141]**. The Nationalist Revolution carried on this struggle. Late in 1914 its leader Sun Yat-sen had even flouted convention by freely marrying his secretary. His bride **Song Qingling** was a member of the remarkable Song family, her five-years younger sister **Song Meiling** marrying Chiang Kai-shek in December 1927.

Song Qingling (1892–1981): Second of the three Song sisters, wife of Sun Yat-sen. American educated, she became Sun's secretary in Japan; they married in 1914. After Sun's death she became identified with the left wing, raising suspicions in the government of Chiang Kai-shek (her brother-in-law). Remained prominent in China under the People's Republic.

In 1931 Chiang Kai-shek's National Government adopted the Family and Inheritance Law. Formulated after extensive study of foreign law, including Japanese, German, Swiss, French and Brazilian, the law was definitely a major advance on tradition. The family was still regarded as patrilinear and patriarchal, with the wife taking her husband's surname and entering his family, and in the case of divorce the father usually received custody of the children, but there was no mention of ancestor worship. The law made women equal in principle with men. It gave women equal right to divorce and allowed them to be family heads. It outlawed bigamy and made no mention of concubinage. Although the system of concubinage persisted in practice, this law was nevertheless a major point in its decline, especially in the cities.

One point of particular importance was that the 1931 Law allowed young people to choose their own spouses. In the cities many young people married without asking their parents' approval of their spouse, showing that the law had some effect. On the other hand, arranged marriages still remained common in the cities, and all but universal in the countryside.

Song Meiling (1897–2003): Youngest of the famous Song sisters and wife of Chiang Kai-shek. Raised the status of women during the Republican period and was a very strong and articulate advocate for Nationalist China in the USA, where she lived for several decades after Chiang's death.

Despite the inclusion of traditional family values in the Confucian revival of the mid-1930s, the Nanjing decade carried on the trend towards greater freedom in urban family life. In former times, Confucian morality had propounded the rigid separation of the sexes, but in the 1930s educated young men and women worked together to some extent and spent their leisure hours together, reading the same books. Young lovers were a common sight in the parks of Shanghai. Although single mothers still suffered social opprobrium, discrimination against them was less savage than in the past.

THE POSITION OF WOMEN, 1900–27

In traditional Confucian China, the status of women was very low indeed. One of the main signs of this was foot-binding, an erotic practice originating in the tenth century. In her bestseller *Wild Swans*, Jung Chang (1991: 31) describes how her great-grandmother had wound a piece of white cloth around the feet of her grandmother, then only two years old. She had bent 'all the toes except the big toe inward and under the sole. Then she placed a large stone on top to crush the arch. My grandmother screamed in agony and begged her to stop', passing out repeatedly from the pain. By the late nineteenth century it is thought that between half and four-fifths of all Han Chinese women had their feet bound, depending on the region of China. Although foot-binding was found among all classes, it was much more prevalent among the upper classes than among peasants, since it was a sign of poor breeding for a girl to have 'big', in other words natural, feet. The Qing court condemned the practice of foot-binding on 1 February 1902 as part of the reforms that followed the Boxer Rebellion. Jung Chang (1991: 32) claims that by 1917 'the practice had virtually been abandoned' in the cities, meaning that girls could grow up with natural feet.

The Revolution of 1911 produced a famous female martyr. Qiu Jin (1875–1907) was an eloquent orator, started a school for girls and spoke out against arranged marriages and foot-binding. She also took charge of a school to train revolutionaries, as a result of which she was arrested by the Qing and, after she refused to divulge secrets despite torture, she was publicly executed in her native city of Shaoxing in Zhejiang Province.

The New Culture Movement saw a surge in attention to the status of women. In her study of women in 'the Chinese Enlightenment', Wang Zheng (1999: 23) speaks of a 'liberal feminist agitation' that was peculiar to this period and exerted a profound impact on the women's movement in China. Public sympathy with feminism grew. Wang specifically rejects the CCP's oft-made claims to have saved Chinese women and even accuses the male proponents of the New Culture Movement of treating women as inferiors in ways that often reflected the old culture rather than the new culture (Wang, 1999: 2, 22). Yet hostility to Confucianism implied supporting women's rights and early in 1916 Chen Duxiu was in the forefront of advocating the emancipation of women. As early as 1919, Mao Zedong, in very passionate and rhetorical language, expressed his support for equality for women (1972: 81). A women's suffrage movement began in 1920, but although it soon split into moderate and revolutionary wings and yielded no successful results for many years, it had at least laid down some kind of foundation. An important point of the New Cultural feminist movement was its association with nationalism and change in general, with many women being prepared to subordinate their identity as women to their patriotism as Chinese.

This association with change and with patriotism was also true of the leftist Nationalist Revolution of the late 1920s, which drew strong support from women and appears to have exercised some effect on their degree of equality, and not just among the educated elite. According to Olga Lang (1946: 105):

> working-class and peasant women, streaming into the trade-unions, peasant unions, the Kuomintang [Nationalist Party] and Communist parties,

and even into the army, joined forces with the educated elite of their sex. Energetic and independent, the women of Canton [Guangzhou] were particularly prominent. These women were treated with great respect by their male comrades and enemies.

(See also Gilmartin, 1995.)

THE POSITION OF WOMEN, 1927–49

Chiang Kai-shek's Nanjing decade, with its anti-leftist momentum, saw a swing against feminism and the women's movement. Lin Yutang was among those to put forward appreciative, but distinctly conservative views on the position of women, their wishes and the demands that should be made upon them, with strong emphasis on their differences from men in terms of functions and the jobs they could undertake **[Doc. 34, p. 142]**. Yet in certain respects the Nanjing decade maintained the trends established during the May Fourth Movement. For instance, education for girls continued to increase (see Chapter 12) and women entered the urban professions, quite a few of them doing very well indeed.

The CCP adopted a very proactive policy towards women. The constitution that the Chinese Soviet Republic adopted in November 1931 (see Chapter 8) guaranteed 'the thorough emancipation of women', recognized freedom of marriage and announced the intention of giving women 'the possibility of participating in the social, economic, political, and cultural life of the entire society' (quoted Brandt, Schwartz and Fairbank, 1971: 223). Quite a few women took part in the Long March.

Women were active during the War Against Japan and after, both among the Nationalist Party and CCP. Although in both cases their role was mainly to support men, this was by no means always the case. Song Meiling took a very active role in promoting women's rights and education and in encouraging women to contribute in every way against the Japanese **[Doc. 35, p. 143]**. She also visited the USA, where she made an extremely favourable impression. In 1943 she became the first Chinese woman, indeed only the second of all women, to address a joint session of the Congress.

The CCP's women's associations were more highly organized for social work than their Nationalist Party counterparts. Their actions included freeing concubines, closing down brothels, informing women of their rights, freeing them from obligations derived from arranged marriages and encouraging them to join the revolution. Membership of the women's associations in the CCP-held areas grew enormously, being only 130,000 in 1927 but some 7.11 million in 1946 (Snow, 1967: 225). One particularly well-known woman to live and work in Yan'an with the CCP was the novelist Ding Ling (1904–86), who is discussed in Chapter 13.

Although it had declined enormously before 1927 and was an absolutely anathema to CCP women, foot-binding was still practised in the countryside as late as 1937. Helen Foster Snow (1967: 223) records her surprise, during a visit to the Communist capital Yan'an in that year, at finding 'the tiniest stumps of bound feet in all China' and, even more astounding, that 'girl children still were being put into bandages in the region', including in Yan'an itself. According to an exhibition entitled 'Enduring Beauty' at the National Museum of Malaysia in Kuala Lumpur in August 1992, a census figure of 1932–3 in the single province of Shanxi found no less than 949,698 women under thirty years of age still with bound feet. Even in the year 2006, the author saw one ancient woman with bound feet in Beijing. Yet the fact remains that when the twentieth century began this horrible custom was inflicted on most small girls, but was virtually dead by 1949.

Despite these clear advances, the rise in the status of females was extremely uneven. Olga Lang (1946: 259) writes that 'girl slavery, though it was illegal, was still common in prewar China, especially in the South'. In his famous novel *Family* (*Jia*), completed in 1931, **Ba Jin** (discussed in Chapter 13) contrasts the style and personality of two young women: one of the educated classes, vibrant and confident, the other a family slave, depressed and frightened, pushed around by everybody and treated with contempt **[Doc. 36, p. 144]**. In the countryside, the incipient changes wrought by the peasants' associations failed to maintain their momentum. By the time the Nationalist Party fell, the lot of most women, especially those of the countryside, was still quite miserable and their status very low.

Ba Jin (pen-name of Li Yaotang, 1904–2005): A leading Chinese novelist of the twentieth century. His best work was a tragic trilogy about a declining high-class but old-fashioned family. The first novel of the trilogy, *Family* (*Jia*), completed in 1931, is among the best novels of twentieth-century China.

RELIGION

The Chinese tradition of religious tolerance survived intact in the first half of the twentieth century. Buddhism, Daoism and the traditional folk religions continued to exercise a powerful hold over the people. Islam existed everywhere, but was prevalent in the west, especially among the Turkic peoples of Xinjiang. Both Islam and Buddhism underwent revival movements. In the case of the Sinic Muslims called Hui this was caused by 'accelerated exchange between China and the outside world', Chinese Muslims beginning to travel extensively in the Islamic centre of Southwest Asia (Gladney, 1991: 53–4). Buddhism produced some significant leaders and theologians, the most eminent among them being probably the reformer Taixu (1890–1957), who tried to harmonize Buddhism with modern science and philosophy and was active in promoting the social welfare function of Buddhism (Welch, 1968). On the other hand, there was a general decline of indigenous religions at the expense of modern secular ideologies and Christianity, especially in the cities. Younger people often scorned their parents' belief in the Buddhist Goddess of Mercy, Guanyin **[Doc. 33, p. 141]**, or in traditional gods of various kinds.

One religion that certainly grew fast in the first half of the twentieth century was Christianity. This was the heyday of the Western Christian missionaries in China, whose influence was considerable not only through the churches they established but also through hospitals and, above all, educational institutions. A survey carried out among both Christian and non-Christian colleges and high schools in the mid-1930s found those with no religion in the majority in all categories of institutions, but Christianity the most popular religion even in non-Christian colleges, although not in non-Christian high schools (Lang, 1946: 359–62). Chiang Kai-shek and his wife Song Meiling were both Christians. Missionary schools were at the forefront of providing education for girls, as Song Meiling rightly pointed out in a major speech on 6 May 1937 **[Doc. 35, p. 143]**.

The May Fourth Movement and the Nationalist Revolution were both hostile to religions of all kinds. Even in the 1930s many prominent people declared themselves agnostic and opposed to religions. Christianity was frequently attacked as the religion of the imperialists. The government even adopted rules against religious propaganda in educational institutions, though these were to some extent ignored.

SECULAR IDEOLOGY

Traditional Confucianism was mainly a secular ideology based on such ethical values as filial piety and loyalty, with a strong hierarchy in which the higher (and older) should show magnanimity towards the lower (and younger) in return for obedience and respect. It also had a strong ceremonial and religious aspect, its rituals being very important in state affairs, and its temples being found everywhere in China.

Confucianism was in strong decline in the first half of the twentieth century. Although conservatives tried to maintain Confucian ritual and Yuan Shikai even performed a sacrificial ceremony to heaven at the Temple of Heaven in Beijing in December 1914, the overthrow of the monarchy dealt Confucianism a fatal blow as a formal ritual or religion. By the 1930s most of the Confucian temples throughout the country had been taken over as schools, museums or for other purposes. In the meantime progressives attacked Confucian ideology as backward and oppressive. As noted in Chapter 5, the May Fourth Movement was extremely hostile to Confucianism and everything it stood for **[Doc. 12, p. 126]**, and the nationalist movement of the 1920s carried on this anti-Confucian drive.

Yet this did not mean that Confucianism as a secular system of moral beliefs died out. On the contrary, it proved extremely tenacious, especially in the countryside. When Chiang Kai-shek swung against the left, he also returned to an appreciation of modernized Confucian values. In February 1934 he launched a campaign called the New Life Movement, which aimed to promote Confucian virtue and moral regeneration and to militarize the nation. It gave great weight to traditional family values and promoted traditional virtues such as politeness, righteousness and integrity, as well as emphasising courtesy, punctuality and hygiene. The military training that was part of the New Life Movement reflected a distinctly fascist tendency, with the Blue Shirts (mentioned in Chapter 7) being prominent in its implementation. Its targets included opium and foot-binding, and, though it held up some aspects of the West for emulation, such as their patriotism and probity in public life, it also tended to blame the West for many of China's evils, believing Western women too free and feminism injurious to family life and feminine morality. Proponents of the combination of tradition and modernity in attitudes towards morality included such people as Lin Yutang, whose works exercised considerable influence in the West **[Doc. 37, p. 145]**.

Sun Yat-sen's three principles of the people (see Chapter 6) naturally retained their influence, becoming a formal part of Chiang Kai-shek's ideology (see Chapter 7). Nationalism became increasingly fervent among many groups of society as Japan strengthened its influence and its determination to take over China became more obvious. Although he called himself nationalist, and the party he led retained that name, Chiang Kai-shek did not benefit much from this nationalist surge, simply because, until the Xi'an Incident discussed in Chapter 9, many of the most ardent Chinese nationalists saw his regime as far too compromising with the Japanese.

Marxism-Leninism exerted considerable influence in the years following the May Fourth Movement. This was most evident in the number of thinkers who led or joined the CCP (see Chapter 8), among whom Mao Zedong has proved most influential in the legacy he has left (see Knight, 2007). The labour movement in the cities and the peasant associations in the countryside had their heyday in the mid-1920s, gaining many supporters fighting for workers' and peasants' rights (Chesneaux, 1968). Even in the 1930s the dialectical materialist way of viewing the world retained some influence among the intelligentsia.

12

Education and the Student Movement

The education system that successive governments developed in the first half of the twentieth century was explicitly nationalist in its aims. And nationalism was the dominant force behind the successive student movements of the period, beginning with the May Fourth Movement (see Chapter 5). Yet the fact remains that the nationalisms displayed in these two forces were at odds with each other. The nationalism the students saw in the education system seemed to them very self-serving and occasionally even traitorous. The main reason for this was that governments appeared to the students to be far too compromising with imperialism, especially Japanese imperialism, and with unhealthy, oppressive and unmodern traditions **[Docs 38 and 39, pp. 146 and 147]**.

THE EDUCATION SYSTEM

One of the main reforms to follow the Boxer Rebellion (see Chapter 3) was the abolition of the traditional examination system by an imperial edict of 2 September 1905. Since these examinations, with all their stereotyped Confucian demands, had for centuries been the main avenue into the ruling mandarinate, the effect of their abolition on society and education was very profound. Henceforth, new avenues and new ideas opened up, and new kinds of people enjoyed opportunities previously denied them, while those brought up with the old Confucian ideas could no longer access the privileges they had earlier taken for granted. Traditional Confucian education declined along with the disappearance of the examinations, and was replaced by more practical systems, heavily influenced by ideas coming originally from the West.

Aims and content of the education system

Early in September 1912 the new Republican government stated the aims of its education system as being to develop a moral sense among students, as well as technical and military training. However, the May Fourth Movement, assisted by a visit to China in mid-1919 by the influential American educationalist John Dewey (1859–1952), pushed for a more American style of education. A presidential mandate of 1922 included the development of individuality among its aims, and also laid down a system with six years of primary and six of secondary schooling.

Chiang Kai-shek's government adopted different aims again. In 1929 the National Government promulgated its view of education, in which it gave pride of place to the official ideology and nationalism and the promotion of social harmony **[Doc. 40, p. 148]**. In the following years the government laid down in great detail the curriculum for primary, secondary and vocational education, as well as required standards and textbooks. The primary curriculum consisted of modern standard Chinese, called *guoyu*, literally 'the national language', citizenship, hygiene, society, nature, arithmetic, fine arts and music. The secondary curriculum added such subjects as English, a second foreign language, history, geography and mathematics. Boys took a military subject called *tongzi jun*, meaning literally 'boys' army', while girls did first aid instead.

In addition to the state system, there were also missionary schools and universities and private academies. The former enjoyed a generally better reputation academically than the state schools, but operated under quite stringent rules. For instance, apart from forbidding them to undertake religious propaganda in class, Chiang's National Government also directed that a Chinese must be appointed principal or director of missionary schools. The private academies were the most traditional part of the education system. Yet although they were old-fashioned in style and curriculum, they were at least more independent of the state; the status of their teachers and their academic reputation were both high.

Compulsory education, the extent of education

Compulsory education had been an ideal since the beginning of the twentieth century. In 1902 imperial regulations on primary schools included one requiring all children to receive seven years of education. A series of laws under the Republic led to a 1930 requirement by Chiang Kai-shek's National

Government to implement four years' compulsory education within twenty years, and to a programme in 1935 to wipe out illiteracy by the middle of the century. All these prescriptions were honoured more in the breach than in the observance.

This does not mean, however, that no progress was made. In fact, the first half of the twentieth century saw the establishment, for the first time in Chinese history, of a reasonably comprehensive education system throughout China, which included primary, secondary and tertiary levels and adult education, as well as teacher, medical and other vocational training. The numbers of students who attended these institutions rose significantly as the period progressed. Government figures for primary schools and below in 1932 show 12,223,066 students, the comparable figure for 1945 being 21,831,898 (Pong and Fung, 1985: 171). According to official statistics, the number of secondary school students of all kinds, including vocational and teacher training, was 627,246 in 1936–7, fell sharply when the war began to 389,948 in 1937–8 but rose to 768,533 in 1940–1 (Kwei, 1943: VI, 650).

An important point emerges from the figures. The overall effect of the War Against Japan on the Chinese education system was not collapse, as might have been expected, but unprecedented efforts at expansion. Two processes were evident. One was a campaign in the areas under the control of the National Government to establish a people's school in every village subdivision. A mass education campaign began in March 1940 and succeeded in raising the incidence of basic literacy more rapidly than before 1937. At the same time urban students went to the countryside in greater numbers than before the War in an effort to use their knowledge and skills to spread basic education and undertake propaganda against the Japanese.

Reliable figures on literacy rates are unavailable. One official National Government figure claims that, in the late years of the war, the number of illiterates was of the order of 171 million, accounting for some 38 per cent of the entire population of China (Kwei, 1943: VI, 645). Chinese Communist Party (CCP) figures claim that at the time it rose to power in 1949, illiteracy exceeded 80 per cent (Mackerras and Yorke, 1991: 218). Both figures are tainted with political propaganda. It is, however, possible that a portion of those who had acquired some literacy during the war lost it afterwards, since nobody is claiming that the mass literacy achieved at that time was more than extremely basic.

Education for girls

In traditional China women were excluded from public education. As early as the mid-1840s an Anglican missionary had been the first to open a school for Chinese girls, supporting it from her own income. In August 1906 the new Qing Ministry of Education gave formal government encouragement to female education by laying down rules regulating its implementation. Coeducation in public universities did not begin in China until February 1920, when Peking University took in two female students. According to Chow Tse-tsung's masterly account of the May Fourth Movement, twenty-eight universities and colleges had women students in 1922 (Chow, 1960: 258). The First Nationalist Party Congress of January 1924 laid down equality between the sexes in various spheres, including education. And Chiang Kai-shek's government maintained that position, even though it also added that education for girls should take on a specifically female bent, such as 'preserving the special qualities of motherhood' **[Doc. 40, p. 148]**.

Although girls remained very much in the minority at all levels of the education system, there were nevertheless advances in the 1930s and 1940s. At university level, females were only 2.5 per cent of tertiary-level students in 1923, but the proportion had risen to about 15 per cent in 1934 and 17.8 per cent in 1947 (Pong and Fung, 1985: 171). In 1935 there were 106,075 girls enrolled in high schools, making up about one-fifth of the total, while in the university, teachers' colleges and technical high schools the proportion of female students was 16 per cent, with 6,272 women (Lang, 1946: 104). In the missionary institutions the proportions were higher, with 35.14 per cent of students being female in Catholic colleges, teacher training schools or universities in 1933, the figure in the Protestant counterparts at the same time being 22 per cent. At a national level there were certain disciplines where women concentrated, the main one being education.

At lower levels the trend in favour of girls was the same, with the missionary schools again leading the way. In primary schools the 1920s average for girls was some 6 per cent of the total. Government figures put the proportion of girl students at or below primary level in 1932 at just over 15 per cent, rising to just over one-quarter at the war's end in 1945. In 1933 Catholic primary school girl students were just over 35 per cent, and nearly 40 per cent were girls in the Protestant schools at about the same time (Pong and Fung, 1985: 171).

The War Against Japan brought more education for women than ever before. In April 1938 the Nationalist Party's Extraordinary Congress laid down that women should be given training 'so that they may be of service to social enterprises and thereby of help to the nation's war strength' (quoted Pong and Fung, 1985: 174). Even in the traditional private academies the number of female students increased during the war, and more dedicated themselves to national service through efforts in public life, rather than simply assisting their own families.

THE STUDENT MOVEMENT

A very important side of education in China in the first half of the twentieth century was a series of student movements, beginning with the May Fourth Movement of 1919, discussed in Chapter 5. Although most of the students' teachers were supportive of the students, the initiative lay generally with the students, not their elders. These were not only student but youth movements. Despite the progress outlined in the previous sections, it was politics, not the education system as a whole, that spawned student protest.

The main stages in the student movement

Following 1919, an early upsurge of the student movement came with the May Thirtieth Movement, the initial incident taking place on 30 May 1925. It saw several thousand university and secondary school students marching into Shanghai's International Settlement to mourn the death of a young Communist trade union leader killed on 15 May by Japanese fire during the suppression of a strike. All political demonstrations were illegal in the International Settlement and many students were arrested, though later released. Later in the day a riot erupted between students and British police, with nine students killed.

On 1 June Shanghai reacted to the May Thirtieth Incident with further demonstrations and a call for a general strike, which resulted in further deaths at the hands of British, Chinese and Japanese police. Meanwhile the movement spread to other cities, with large-scale demonstrations and strikes taking place. For example, on 3 June some 30,000 Beijing students went on strike and demonstrated in resonance with Shanghai counterparts. Not until September was the Shanghai general strike suppressed.

After a further upsurge in 1931 when Japan invaded Manchuria, the next main stage in the student movement came with the December Ninth Movement of 1935. On that day about 2,000 students demonstrated in Beiping (Beijing) to demand resistance to Japan. Soldiers and police broke up the demonstration and arrested a number of people, with injuries resulting. The students decided to go on strike in reaction to this, demanding the release of those arrested, and punishment for police and soldiers who had injured student demonstrators. In the following days the movement spread to other cities, such as Hangzhou, Guangzhou, Shanghai and Xi'an, and another large demonstration took place in Beiping on 16 December. Chiang Kai-shek's National Government shortly took measures to defuse the movement and the students did not win nearly as much support as they had hoped from sectors of society other than the intelligentsia.

There were four 'student waves' (*xuechao*) in the postwar period: in December 1945, late 1946 to early 1947, May and June 1947 and in mid-1948. One authority classifies these student waves as 'essentially an anti-war movement' that focused attention on the conflict between the Nationalist Party and CCP gathering momentum at that time (see Chapter 10) 'and thus became an issue in the politics of the Civil War itself' (Pepper, 1978: 42). The movement took the form of demonstrations, strikes and boycotts. The government, which rightly saw the protests as a threat to its survival, reacted intransigently. Arrests of students were very numerous, and in a number of incidents some were even killed by government police. For example, on 1 December 1945 armed raiders entered the Southwest Associated University in Kunming (the wartime amalgamation of Peking and Qinghua Universities in Beiping and Nankai University of Tianjin), killing at least three students and wounding others. On 5 July 1948 a clash in Beiping between government police and students from northeast China left eighteen students dead and many others wounded.

Issues and significance in the student movement

The overriding factors in the student movement were nationalism and its twin anti-imperialism. The May Thirtieth Movement of 1925 was aimed originally against the Japanese, but it was a British policeman whose actions led to the deaths of Chinese students during the incident itself. As a result, the movement became more generally anti-imperialist. According to Richard Rigby (1980: 178), 'It convinced large numbers of Chinese, particularly in urban areas, that their misfortunes were the result of something called imperialism' on which their miseries could be blamed. More specifically, 1925 was a major point in bringing Chinese people to the view that the solution to their woes lay in abrogating the unequal treaties, the symbol of imperialist oppression.

The prime spur to the student movement of the 1930s was resistance to Japan. Although earlier protests against Japan's invasion of Manchuria in 1931 died down in 1932, it was Japanese incursions that revived them late in 1935. In October 1935 Japanese Foreign Minister Hirota Koki proposed a three-way axis consisting of Japan, China and Manchukoku against communism and to develop north China. Almost immediately afterwards the Japanese instigated an autonomy movement in north China that was patently aimed at increasing their own hold on the region. The December Ninth Movement of 1935 resulted both from Japanese imperialism and was also the forerunner to much more thorough-going national resistance to Japan from the end of 1936 (see Chapter 9).

The postwar student movement became bound up with anti-American and anti-Japanese feeling. In particular, the incident giving rise to the second of the four 'student waves' was the claimed rape by two American marines of Peking University student Shen Chong on 24 December 1946. One of the issues of the last student wave in 1948 was anti-Americanism and the fear that the USA was trying to revive Japanese imperialism.

Right from 1919, the student movement also became bound up with hostility to the prevailing political order and assisted the left substantially. The May Fourth Movement was clearly aimed against the warlord politics of the time. The May Thirtieth Movement (1925) contributed to the Nationalist Revolution and was a highly significant stage in its development. It was most certainly hostile to the warlord politics of the day, and when on 30 May 1926 the Shanghai Student Federation called for the continuation of the struggle, they bemoaned that the situation in north China was worse than ever due to warlord-imperialist collaboration. The May Thirtieth Movement assisted the CCP by contributing to the growth and leadership within its mass movement. According to Rigby (1980: 178), it was at this time also that Mao Zedong became aware of the peasantry's revolutionary potential.

In the case of the December Ninth Movement (1935), students became disgusted with the failure of the National Government to give top priority to resisting Japan. John Israel (1966: 184) describes the relationship of the students with the government in terms not of total alienation, but of 'gradual erosion, or, more aptly, inner decay'. He claims that the CCP infiltrated the movement in its later stages. Some CCP sources express themselves in much more emotive and stronger language in condemning Chiang Kai-shek for his failure to resist Japan and the evil effects Japanese activities were producing on Chinese society **[Doc. 39, p. 147]**. What is not in doubt is that at this time the students' revolution movement veered steadily to the left.

Of all the student movements, it was those that followed the war that were most specifically aimed against the government. Chiang Kai-shek, for his part, believed fiercely that they were being instigated by the CCP, and there is no doubt that left-wing students were actively involved. Government reaction, however, had the effect of turning the students more and more against it, and towards the CCP. One writer claims that the CCP's advocacy of a united front and coalition government won it much credit with the students, even as the Nationalist Party 'was squandering its own fund of popular support' (Pepper, 1978: 93).

The student movements were also catalysts for and contributors to progressive socio-cultural tendencies. Although the May Thirtieth Incident (1925) was student-led, the following months were much more important for their contribution to the Chinese labour than the student movement. The organizers and followers of the December Ninth Movement (1935) saw themselves very much in the tradition of revolution, which had been so important in their lives. While hostility to Japan was the focus of their thinking, they also demanded a more equal society in which the rural masses would be involved. It is not surprising that some of their participants later gained prominence under CCP rule.

The postwar student movement was extremely concerned with economic hardship, the fate of education, government oppression and the rising rate of inflation. Indeed the last two 'student waves' of 1947 and 1948 were very specific that their main targets included hunger and economic misery. And they also demanded an end to civil war and the resumption of peace. Students became increasingly willing to blame the existing authorities for the real woes that the Chinese people were suffering, and it is evident that the loss of confidence symbolized by the continuing movement was one of the reasons why the Nationalist Party fell.

13

Literature and Theatre

The first half of the twentieth century was a creative and innovative one for literature, theatre and the arts. A period of wrenching transformation, it saw the development of major new forms, as well as a change in emphasis among the existing genres. It also saw exponents of traditional forms who wished to change them, as well as those who wanted to cling to tradition desperately, as representing the old Chinese culture they loved so much. This chapter does not attempt to cover all forms of literature, theatre and the arts, since that would need far more than a brief chapter even to scratch the surface. Instead it takes up just a couple of representative forms: fiction and theatre.

SOME BACKGROUND

The traditional Chinese educated elite had very clear ideas about what constituted serious literature. It included the classics and standard histories, as well as essays and high-class poetry. It used a language now called classical Chinese, which itself existed in several styles according to period, purpose of writing and other factors. This literary language was 'characterised by compressed syntax and an elaborate, allusive vocabulary' (McDougall and Louie, 1997: 3).

However, novels and short stories in vernacular language did not come under the heading of serious literature. This was despite the fact that China of the late imperial period (late thirteenth to early twentieth centuries) produced quite a few splendid novels, some of them greatly admired in contemporary times as belonging to the world literary canon. However, those who controlled the literary canon looked down on oral literature, folk songs and poetry as very inferior.

In traditional Chinese drama, song is primary, and in virtually none do performers express themselves entirely in speech. There was an elite form of drama called *Kunqu*, which originated in Kunshan, near Shanghai, in the sixteenth century, and produced some highly regarded works. However, the educated elite regarded the local popular theatre with the greatest contempt, even though it developed to produce some spectacular urban drama genres by the eighteenth and nineteenth centuries. Among these genres by far the best known is the *jingju*, usually translated as **Peking Opera**, which originated in Beijing as a combination of other local styles late in the eighteenth century, and developed to maturity by about the middle of the nineteenth.

Peking Opera: Known nowadays as *jingju* in Chinese, this is the most famous and perhaps most developed of China's traditional theatre genres and probably the nearest to a Chinese national theatre.

The popular local theatre was centred on actors, not authors. Throughout Chinese history, actors have been very low in social status and suffered various forms of legal discrimination. A notable feature of Chinese theatre is that since the Ming dynasty (1368–1644) acting troupes were either all-male, or all-female, mostly the former. Usually it was boys or men who played the female roles (*dan*), individuals not scorning to use them as homosexual lovers, despite their low social status. The nineteenth century saw the rise of a few *jingju* stars.

THEORY OF THE ARTS

In literature and theatre, as in other fields, the twentieth century saw a process of rapid and growing influence from the West, both in theory and form. Models for literary figures tended to come from the West, sometimes through Japan. This impact gathered momentum with the New Culture Movement of the second decade of the century, as shown by the appeal of the two gentlemen, Mr Science and Mr Democracy (see Chapter 5).

One aspect of this influence was that the status of the various kinds of literature and the arts changed greatly in the twentieth century, including in its first half. McDougall and Louie (1997: 2) write: 'The democratisation of the literary canon, of its creation and its audience, has been one of the major achievements of the reformist literary intellectuals in the twentieth century'. No longer was it mandatory for a respectable person to despise fiction and popular drama. These forms of literature came to be more appreciated, even by the intellectual elite. The notion of 'mass arts' began to take root. To be sure, traditional views persisted, but social change rendered them less and less relevant.

A very early example of the reformers was Liang Qichao, whose activities and views have been mentioned earlier (see Chapter 3). In 1902 he wrote of the need for reform in popular literature in order to reform China's politics and morals. His reason was very simple: that popular literature, including both novels and dramas, exercises major influence over people and the way they think and behave **[Doc. 41, p. 148]**.

Liang Qichao's notion became increasingly widespread, even dominant, as the twentieth century progressed. It implied reform both in terms of content and form. Content should reflect the life of the people, and in such a way that it promoted social reform. This idea was taken up vigorously during the New Culture and May Fourth Movements, many proponents demanding that novels and dramas should push such themes as social equality, and the rights of women and youth.

The New Culture thinkers were keen to promote realism in literary works. In the December 1915 issue of the famous journal *Youth Magazine*, mentioned in Chapter 5, Chen Duxiu maintained that 'Our literature and art are still in the ages of classicism and romanticism. From now on the trend should be towards realism. In literature, we should emphasize the truthful recording of facts and events' (quoted Tang, 1993: 2). In a later issue of the same journal he also proposed abandoning classical Chinese and writing in a much simpler, popular style that would be accessible to a much wider audience **[Doc. 42, p. 149]**.

Some still believed that the old genres and writing styles of literature should be maintained. The argument was that these literary forms were the genuine representatives of China's tradition and their disappearance would mean the destruction of Chinese culture. One example illustrating the persistence of this kind of thinking was the 1928 publication of the *Draft History of the Qing (Qingshi gao)*. This work was exactly in the style of the old dynastic histories, the succeeding dynasty recording the entire history of its predecessor. But the *Draft History of the Qing* remained a draft. It was never accepted as a formal 'standard history' (*zhengshi*). The implication was clear: some might resist change, but a return to the pure authentic tradition of the past was not really a viable option.

Chiang Kai-shek's conservatism in all fields failed to dent what had become the mainstream theory on literature and the arts, and examples illustrating this trend will be given below. The most radical theory came from Chiang Kai-shek's opponents on the left, the most noted being of course Mao Zedong. In May 1942, as part of the Rectification Movement discussed in Chapter 8, Mao convened a forum on literature and the arts in Yan'an, and attempted to map out a detailed theory of the nature and purpose of the arts.

Mao put forward several major ideas. The first was that literature and the arts must be a propaganda tool within the revolution, pushing forward the revolution and the interests of the classes at the bottom of society, especially the workers and peasants. In Doc. 43 he refers several times to literature and the arts as 'cogs and wheels' in the revolutionary machine and mentions the class nature of all art [**Doc. 43, p. 149**]. Second, Mao was very keen to integrate form and content and propounded that propaganda should not sacrifice artistry. In theory, it should be possible to create good art that was also propaganda. Still, experience suggested that if there was a clash between the two, it was artistry that would have to give way. Third, Mao took the idea of mass art to great lengths. He hated the elitist art that had formerly been so dominant. The audience for the art created in the Communist-held areas would not be the urban-educated bourgeoisie but the masses of workers and peasants [**Doc. 44, p. 150**].

FICTION

Along with drama, fiction was the form chosen by the best new writers to express their political and social ideas. One authoritative work attributes this partly to Liang Qichao, 'who was influenced by the Japanese debate on the political novel at the end of the nineteenth century' (McDougall and Louie, 1997: 82). We have seen that this factor went hand in hand with a rise in status of fiction. For the best writers to choose fiction as their medium was new to the twentieth century. The period also saw some innovations in the form of fiction. One of these was the use of the diary format, which allowed the diarist to comment or express emotions about the narrative.

The dominant form of fiction from the New Culture Movement to the end of the 1920s was the short story (*duanpian xiaoshuo*). The most distinguished representative of this genre and probably the foremost literary figure in modern China was Lu Xun (1881–1936), the pen-name of Zhou Shuren. Beginning with 'Diary of a Madman' ('Kuangren riji'), published in *New Youth* in May 1918, Lu Xun wrote a series of some thirty short stories, the aim of which was to castigate the hypocrisy of Chinese traditional society, with equally sharp barbs directed against contemporary times. 'Diary of a Madman' shows the inner thoughts of somebody who believes those around him want to eat him. The symbolism is that Chinese society is cannibalistic and in great need of thorough-going transformation towards justice. The madman looks towards the day when the man-eating society will disappear, and the final words of the story are: 'save the children'.

Perhaps Lu Xun's best work is 'The True Story of A Q' ('A Q zhengzhuan'), which was written between December 1921 and February 1922. Through a lowly peasant's career and eventual execution on fraudulent grounds, Lu Xun gives a highly satirical view of the 1911 Revolution for having made no difference at all to the sufferings of the poor. The Chinese ruling elite comes over as hypocritical, self-serving and heartless, while only among the downtrodden and impoverished classes is there anything remotely resembling decency.

Lu Xun was a leading force in the establishment of the League of Left-Wing Writers in March 1930, a body that included most of the leading leftist writers of the day. Lu Xun made a speech at the inaugural meeting advocating the use of literature to promote revolution. The League tended to dominate literary debate in the 1930s, pushing opinion towards the left. This was the period when government inaction in the face of Japanese encroachments made patriotism and opposition to the government a related, even single, cause.

It is obvious that Lu Xun was a strong supporter not of gradual but of revolutionary change. Because of his literary distinction and views, he attracted praise from the CCP. In particular Mao Zedong's verdict of Lu Xun was fulsome: 'he was not only a great man of letters but a great thinker and revolutionary' (Mao, 1965: II, 372).

In the 1930s the full-length novel (*changpian xiaoshuo*) emerged as the main form of fiction, though good short stories continued to attract wide readership. The foremost fiction writers of the two decades leading up to the CCP's victory were Ba Jin (pen-name of Li Yaotang, 1904–2005), Mao Dun (pen-name of Shen Yanbing, 1896–1981), Lao She (pen-name of Shu Qingchun, 1899–1966) and Ding Ling (pen-name of Jiang Bingzhi, 1904–86), all very left-wing in their sympathies. Their works tend to be autobiographical and focus on social problems, especially those associated with women and the family.

An excellent representative series is Ba Jin's *Torrents, A Trilogy* (*Jiliu, Sanbuqu*). It consists of three novels, *Family* (*Jia*), completed in 1931; *Spring* (*Chun*), which came out in 1938; and *Autumn* (*Qiu*), published in 1940. The novels trace the decline and disintegration of the old-fashioned Gao family and the eventual tragedies that befall its members, including suicide and broken marriages. One literary critic of the People's Republic writes of the trilogy: 'It reveals the inner workings and collapse of the feudal patriarchal system and the rebellion of young people against the family' (Tang, 1993: 284). An extract revealing something of the nature of the first novel, *Family*, is given in Doc. 36 [**Doc. 36, p. 144**].

Of the four writers mentioned above, one is a woman, Ding Ling, and we might take her as a representative of the female authors emerging in the 1930s. She actually joined the CCP in 1932 and as a result was arrested in 1933, and then kept in detention for three years. On her release she went to join the CCP forces, being greeted by Mao Zedong. Her loyalty did not save her when the Rectification Movement erupted in 1942, and she was heavily criticised, though she continued to write. Her main pre-1949 works included the novel *Mother* (*Muqin*), published in 1933, and *The Sun Shines*

Over the Sanggan River (*Taiyang zhao zai Sanggan he shang*), written and published in 1948. The first of these two novels deals with the political and personal independence struggle of her own mother. The second is based on her personal experiences and reflects the life of the peasants during the land reform in north China. Despite the criticism she had suffered during the Rectification Campaign, the novel was very well regarded by the CCP and won a Stalin Prize in 1951.

While focusing on the mainstream short-story writers and novelists who emphasised social causes, social injustice and left-wing political struggle, we should not forget that there was a more conservative school of writers who eschewed such themes. In the 1930s several major figures were strongly opposed to the idea that literature should be simply an arm of politics and promoter of revolution. They even included Zhou Zuoren (1885–1967), who was Lu Xun's younger brother.

Many of the apolitical novels are written in classical Chinese, which shows that their target audience belonged to the educated elite. Themes included love stories, with some ending happily, especially in good marriages and marital harmony. The best exponent of this kind of novel was Zhang Henshui (1895–1967), whose fiction was widely read 'partly because of its reliance on traditional modes of narrative, characterisation and plot' (McDougall and Louie, 1997: 105). Another kind of conservative fiction was the knight-errant or martial arts novel, with its world of fantasy so totally different from the realism advocated by people like Chen Duxiu. The best writer in this genre was Xiang Kairan (1890–1957), author of over twenty novels, the most famous being *Modern Tales of Chivalrous Heroes* (*Jindai xiayi yingxiong zhuan*). His chivalrous heroes are patriotic and the novel ends in the defeat of foreigners, Japanese and Europeans. Though traditional in theme and remote from social injustice, it is in that sense not entirely apolitical.

THEATRE

In the first half of the twentieth century Chinese theatre shows facets similar to those we find in fiction. There was a tension between the tradition and the modern impulses that came largely from Western influence. There were also some differences. By far the most important was that several completely new forms of drama arose in the first half of the twentieth century and they continued to mould Chinese theatre under the People's Republic.

By far the most important of these new forms is called the 'spoken drama' (*huaju*), which we can define as 'modern or Western-style drama in which the spoken word is primary' (Trapido, 1985: 395), as opposed to the mainly sung traditional theatre. The item most scholars regard as the first Chinese 'spoken drama' was an adaptation by Chinese authors of American Harriett Beecher Stowe's novel *Uncle Tom's Cabin* attacking slavery. Entitled *The Black Slave's Cry to Heaven* (*Heinu yutian lu*), it was first performed in Tokyo in 1907 and later the same year in Shanghai. As the title shows, it already embodied a feature that was to become very prominent in later spoken dramas, namely that it was a piece of social criticism on behalf of the downtrodden in society **[Doc. 45, p. 150]**. Another important feature of spoken drama was the use of vernacular language.

The New Culture and May Fourth Movements gave great inspiration to the spoken drama. In June 1918, *New Youth* devoted a whole issue to the famous Norwegian realist dramatist Henrik Ibsen (1828–1906), whose social critiques were something of a model to Chinese writers. An early spoken drama spawned by the New Culture Movement was *Zhongsheng dashi* (*The Greatest Event in Her Life*), by Hu Shi, published in 1919. Based in some ways on Ibsen's *A Doll's House*, it deals with a young woman's demand to choose her own husband, rather than allowing her parents arrange a marriage for her **[Doc. 33, p. 141]**. As we saw in Chapter 5, Hu was a leading liberal thinker of the time.

The May Fourth period gave rise to numerous drama societies, each with their own approach to theatre. The 1920s produced a range of good spoken dramas on such themes as women's emancipation, with the left wing dominating strongly. However, the spoken drama reached its highest point in the few years leading up to the War Against Japan.

Cao Yu (pen-name of Wan Jiabao, 1910–96): 'China's Shakespeare'. Regarded as the best dramatist of the 'spoken drama', a new form of theatre introduced into China in 1907. Cao Yu's best plays date from the 1930s; his masterpiece *Thunderstorm* (*Leiyu*) was published in 1934 and premiered in 1935.

The best exponent was **Cao Yu** (pen-name of Wan Jiabao), who is sometimes dubbed the 'Shakespeare of China' (Jonathan Noble in Leiter, 2007: 78) and is universally acknowledged as China's best twentieth-century playwright. Though he wrote quite a bit under the People's Republic, his early plays stand out, being noted for their powerful social criticism and mastery of language and characterization. It is perhaps ironic that his first play *Thunderstorm* (*Leiyu*), published in 1934 and premiered the next year, is generally regarded as his best. *Thunderstorm* is about the themes of family relationships and capitalist exploitation. The lead character is the manager of a successful coalmine but, though he imagines himself as a fine example of a Westernized Confucian patriarch, he succeeds in ruining the lives of his family and employees through his insensitivity. The action takes place over just a few hours, reaching a harrowing and tragic climax against the background of a gathering thunderstorm, which bursts out at the end of the third act of four, the 'hiss of rain' forming a dramatic backdrop to the last act.

During the War Against Japan, theatre was a widely used and effective propaganda tool. In particular, the CCP enthusiastically exploited theatre to stir feeling against the Japanese and class enemies. One drama worth mentioning is *The White-Haired Girl*, which was premiered in April 1945 at the CCP's Seventh Party Congress. With its theme of the victorious class struggle of a tenant's daughter against a landlord, this item is very direct in its propaganda on behalf of the peasant masses and of downtrodden women [**Doc. 46, p. 151**]. It is notable for another reason: it is an early full-scale Chinese example of a form called *geju* or 'sung drama', which is equivalent to Western opera but almost always adopts Chinese stories and melodies, with the orchestra containing not only Western but also Chinese instruments. Acting and costumes are in the realist tradition, quite unlike the traditional Chinese theatre.

As for these traditional forms, some did reasonably well in the first half of the twentieth century, while others, notably the formerly elite *Kunqu*, came near to extinction. *Jingju*, or Peking Opera, enjoyed a kind of heyday. Quite a few people, both in China and overseas, came to accept it as China's 'national drama' (*guoju*). This period also saw the height of the career of several outstanding Peking Opera performers, the best known of them, and by far the most famous actor China has ever produced, being **Mei Lanfang**.

It is not surprising that traditional theatre should have come under somewhat less influence from the West than the new forms or that many of its enthusiasts clung to it as the representative of Chinese culture. Traditional stories, modes of acting, music and staging remained prevalent. Mei Lanfang and several other well-known actors belonged to the traditional category of male *dan*, that is men who play the roles of women, whereas in the spoken drama actors played people of their own sex.

Yet modernity profoundly affected Peking Opera. One scholar even describes it as 'a modern construction' greatly affected 'by the conditions of colonial modernity' (Goldstein, 2007: 3). Although the centrality of the actor remained, we find the beginnings of what are called 'newly written historical dramas' (*xinbian lishi ju*). What this means is that authors wrote scripts for plays designed to last two or three hours and that rose to a climax and denouement in the Western (modern) fashion, not with the structure of traditional times in which short episodes lasting less than an hour were presented. Mei Lanfang performed several dramas written specially for him by theatre scholar Qi Rushan (1877–1962). Mei himself also performed in Peking Opera with content reflecting social criticism, for example *Waves of the Sea of Sin* (*Niehai bolan*) (1914), a long drama dealing with the evils of prostitution. The context of Peking Opera was transformed in the first half of the twentieth century. For instance, the large modern proscenium stage set opposite the audience in a theatre began to replace the traditional square stage with the audience sitting on three sides in a teahouse or guildhall or in

Mei Lanfang (1894–1961): Probably twentieth-century China's greatest actor and exponent of China's traditional drama genre *Jingju* (Peking Opera). Unrivalled in the male *dan* roles – the parts of women played by men. The first prominent Chinese actor to perform abroad, visiting Japan, the Soviet Union and the USA.

the open air. Another modern phenomenon was that Chinese theatre began to be internationalized. Mei Lanfang was the most widely known overseas, visiting Japan, the USA and Europe, but was not the only Peking Opera actor of that time to go abroad.

Part 4

CONCLUSION

14

Conclusion and Evaluation

A mong many approaches to evaluating the first half of the twentieth century in China, two only are considered here, involving two central questions. These are:

- Just how significant is this period in the long haul of Chinese history?
- How should one assess the achievements of the period and its leaders?

In addition to approaching these two questions briefly, this chapter will suggest in outline some reasons why the period ended with the victory of the CCP in China.

SIGNIFICANCE OF THE PERIOD 1900–49

Many factors lead to the conclusion that the period 1900–49 was of enormous significance in Chinese history, of which five are offered here. While these are clearly related to each other, they are also separate.

In the first place, the extent of change was greater than over any earlier half-century in Chinese history. It is true that China had undergone radical change at previous times, notably in the second half of the third century BC with the unification of China and founding of its first fully fledged state under Qin Shihuang, and in the thirteenth century with the Mongol conquest. Yet at no time had such decisively new ideas, political and economic forms and cultural and social notions been introduced simultaneously into China as in the first half of the twentieth century. While beneath these processes there were also vast areas of continuity, change had never been so drastic.

Second, this was the period that saw the overthrow of the monarchy. The imperial system of government had survived unchanged since the third century BC when introduced by the Qin dynasty, and even before that by monarchs and princes. Although the system of official bureaucracy had evolved substantially over the centuries, the basic system of monarchical government, with an authoritarian and hierarchical mandarinate and underpinned with Confucian ideology, was extremely ancient in China. The significance of its overthrow, which at the beginning of the twenty-first century appears permanent, can hardly be exaggerated.

Third, the period saw the first serious flowering of those forces we associate with modernity. Nationalism was not only a major theme in this half century but also fairly new to it. While love of China and its culture and people was very ancient, that kind of dedication to nation so important in the modern world had hardly taken shape when the twentieth century dawned but was enormously powerful by 1949. In economic terms, industry remained extremely backward and concentrated in particular areas, but it was in this period that it made a serious beginning. Although the origin of railways, to take but one major example of infrastructure and communications, lay in the nineteenth century, the beginnings were very tentative then, with the early twentieth century seeing vast acceleration. In socio-cultural terms, this period saw a real flowering of modern ideas and literary forms and styles, as well as a completely new modern education system, and was also when the ancient custom of foot-binding was virtually eradicated for young girls.

Fourth, this period was one of upheaval and renewal, seeing an occupation among the most disastrous and destructive in China's long history and ending with the dawn of a decisive regeneration. It was not only the Qing dynasty but Chinese civilization as a whole that was in serious decline in the nineteenth century. Despite the reforms of the Qing's last decade, this overall decline continued into the warlord period, but there was cultural renaissance in the May Fourth Movement (1919). The beginnings of regeneration under Chiang Kai-shek were aborted by the War Against Japan. Of all foreign occupations in Chinese history, only the Mongol of the thirteenth century was clearly more devastating for China than the Japanese. But in sharp contrast to the Mongols, the Japanese failed to conquer China, weak and disorganized as it was. On the contrary, for a variety of reasons, China was able to defeat the occupation. The succeeding period of yet further war gave no joy to the incumbent government, but did result in a more sustained period of regeneration for China from 1949 onwards, the results of which are still evident in the early twenty-first century.

Finally, and in sum, the period 1900–49 saw three major political revolutions. These were that of 1911, which overthrew the monarchy, the Nationalist Revolution of 1925–7, which brought Chiang Kai-shek's National Government to power, and the Communist Revolution, which climaxed in the establishment of the People's Republic of China in October 1949. While China underwent processes before the twentieth century that can be judged as revolutionary, no preceding half-century had seen so many revolutions. Given the importance of change in the concept of revolution, this fact alone comes near to justifying the summation of this period as 'China in transformation'.

EVALUATION OF THE ACHIEVEMENTS AND LEADERS OF THE PERIOD

To say that a period is of enormous historical significance does not mean that it was a good period for the ordinary person to be alive. Indeed, the first half of the twentieth century was fraught with tragedy for the Chinese people. Yet there were also achievements amid these tragedies, some of them already referred to in this conclusion. These include the overthrow of the millennia-old monarchy that still held great political power, the establishment of a new political order, the beginnings of a modern economy and education system, and a certain degree of cultural renewal and social progress.

There were many failures as well. Having succeeded in his revolution Sun Yat-sen was forced to see his own achievement appropriated and betrayed by Yuan Shikai. It is true that he tried once again in south China and secured an enormously high reputation, one he still holds. But even his southern Guangzhou regime encountered warlord and other resistance that made its achievements rather meagre. Most historians nowadays take a rather restrained view of the influence Sun exerted over his times.

Neither Sun nor even Chiang Kai-shek succeeded in suppressing the war-lords fully, nor in gaining full control over more than a relatively small part of China's overall territory. In economic terms, the lot of the average person was probably worse at the end of Chiang Kai-shek's rule than it had been at the beginning. Although Chiang Kai-shek himself was reasonably honest, his officials and government became more and more corrupt, until only a minor-ity mourned his departure. And while his government effected some social improvements, it is quite possible to argue that Chinese society was just so unequal and so unjust that Chiang should have given social issues a far higher priority than in fact he did. The wretched of the earth gained very little indeed from his administration, and when he fell in 1949 slavery still existed in the country and drug addiction was rampant.

In evaluating the achievements of any period, it is necessary to remember both the criteria its leaders establish for it and the international and domestic contexts within which it works. Given the forces Sun found himself against, and his very limited military backing, was it really feasible for him to do better in the long haul? Perhaps what is remarkable is not that his revolutions failed but that he succeeded in overthrowing the monarchy at all.

While it is true that the ideals and realities of Chiang Kai-shek's National Government were hopelessly at variance with each other, the fact that he continued to face Japanese aggression from abroad and opposition at home from warlords and the CCP, and even from within his own Nationalist Party, perhaps reduces the extent of the harsh judgement a historian might cast on him. Given his own conservative lights, he perhaps did the best he could under the circumstances in which he found himself. Of course we shall never know, but a continuing field of interesting speculation is whether any other leader or party could have coped better with China's problems. For instance, would the CCP have done a better job had it won in 1927 instead of 1949?

REASONS FOR THE DEFEAT OF THE NATIONALIST PARTY

Yet the fact remains that Chiang Kai-shek finished the War Against Japan seriously weakened, and that he fell soon afterwards, despite the international support he still enjoyed. And the question why is an inescapable one. The reasons are economic, social and political, among others. They cover not only why Chiang lost, but take us to territory considering why Mao Zedong and his CCP won.

The fact is that Chiang's China faced disintegration in the late 1940s because devastation from the war and out-of-control inflation were bringing the economy to the point of total collapse. With the fall of the economy came social disorder. Not only did the CCP lead the peasantry against the Nationalists, but the intelligentsia and other urban groupings turned against Chiang and his regime to a very significant extent, while the postwar student movements added several nails to the coffin of his regime. Meanwhile corruption ate away at his party's strength and vigour. Despite its rhetoric, it became a tired body more interested in itself than in the people, bereft of coherent and interesting ideas capable of bringing about a further regeneration. The USA remained more or less loyal to Chiang, but in the years immediately following the War Against Japan was certainly in no mood to offer that kind of military, economic or other help that had any chance at all of saving him against the CCP.

On the other side of the coin, historians have debated why the CCP proved so strong, especially following its disastrous collapse at the hands of Chiang Kai-shek 1927. In 1971, in the era of the Vietnam War and radical Western scholarship on Asia, historian Mark Selden published an influential account in which he argued that the CCP's strength lay primarily in its ability to lead the social revolution, what he termed 'the Yan'an way'. He credited it with 'a bold and creative attack on problems of rural oppression and disintegration' during the War Against Japan (Selden, 1971: 120). As Mao Zedong's reputation has declined, this view has come under challenge, and Selden's 1995 revised edition withdraws from the enthusiasm evident in the original. Yet it remains possible that the Communists' ability to carry out radical social activity in the countryside constituted a reason why they were able to attract peasant support.

Another school of thought contended that peasant nationalism during the War Against Japan was the primary impetus for the CCP's success. In 1962 Chalmers Johnson advanced the thesis that the CCP's reform efforts in Jiangxi had been failures. What really gave it the opportunity to invigorate itself was the ability to unite with the peasants in a nationalist defensive war against the Japanese. Whereas peasants had been relatively acquiescent in their lot up to this point, the Japanese invasion really galvanized them to political activism, and it was the CCP that benefited (Johnson, 1962: especially 69–70). This view lays very little emphasis on the aspect of social revolution. It also implies that, without the War Against Japan, the CCP might never have won, leaving the Nationalist Party in power.

In a highly thoughtful and analytical essay, Suzanne Pepper (2004) has surveyed the vast literature on the CCP's victory and especially Johnson's thesis that it has its root in peasant nationalism spawned by resistance to Japan. Among a myriad other points she notes that Mao himself expressed gratitude to a visiting Japanese Socialist Party delegation in 1964 because the Japanese invasion had made the CCP's victory possible: 'Had your imperial army not invaded more than half of China, the Chinese people would not have been able to unite to oppose you, and the CCP would not have been able to seize state power' (Pepper, 2004: 119). She criticizes Johnson for being too monocausal, for attributing too much to peasant nationalism to the exclusion of many other major factors. However, she essentially finds that the concept of peasant nationalism has stood the test of time pretty well and is likely to remain important in debates about twentieth-century Chinese history (see also Mackerras, 1989: 158–60).

The question of whether the CCP would have won had the Japanese never invaded China is likely to go on intriguing historians indefinitely. But the fact remains that the Second World War, of which China's War of Resistance Against Japan was so significant a part, left the globe as a whole transformed, not merely China. Was the gigantic series of events that was that Second World War inevitable anyway, and if it had not happened, would Japan have remained for long the power it had become by the 1930s? Speculation on such matters is interesting and possibly instructive, but leads us into the realm of such grand historical theories as inevitability, which are well outside the scope of this small volume. What is perhaps most important is that China did fight and win a war against Japan between 1937 and 1945, that Chiang Kai-shek did fight and lose a civil war against the CCP from 1946 to 1949, and that the CCP did establish its People's Republic of China (PRC) in October 1949.

Part 5

DOCUMENTS

Document 1   THE REPUBLICAN PERIOD

This is a summary of the Republican period by the late John King Fairbank, one of the most distinguished twentieth-century historians of China in the English-speaking world. In it he states some central themes of the period of the Republic of China.

The 37 years from 1912 to 1949 . . . were marked by civil war, revolution and invasion at the military-political level, and by change and growth in the economic, social, intellectual and cultural spheres . . .

China's modern problem of adjustment has been that of a dominant, majority civilization that rather suddenly found itself in a minority position in the world. Acceptance of outside 'modern' ways was made difficult by the massive persistence of deeply-rooted Chinese ways. The issue of outer versus inner absorbed major attention at the time and still confronts historians as a thorny problem of definition and analysis.

Anyone comparing the Chinese Republic of 1912–49 with the late Ch'ing [Qing] period that preceded it or with the People's Republic that followed will be struck by the degree of foreign influence upon and even participation in Chinese life during these years. The Boxer peace settlement of 1901 had marked the end of blind resistance to foreign privilege under the unequal treaties; students flocked to Tokyo, Peking proclaimed foreign-style reforms, and both weakened the old order. After the Revolution of 1911 the outside world's influence on the early republic is almost too obvious to catalogue: the revolutionaries avoided prolonged civil war lest it invite foreign intervention; they tried in 1912 to inaugurate a constitutional, parliamentary republic based on foreign models; President Yuan Shih-kai's [Shikai's] foreign loans raised controversy; the New Culture movement after 1917 was led by scholars returned from abroad; the May Fourth movement of 1919 was triggered by power politics at Versailles; the Chinese Communist Party (CCP) was founded in 1921 under Comintern prompting; Sun Yat-sen reorganized the Kuomintang (KMT) [Nationalist Party] after 1923 with Soviet help; the Nationalist Revolution 1925–27 was inspired by patriotic anti-imperialism. Truly, the early republic was moved by foreign influences that were almost as pervasive as the Japanese invasion was to become after 1931.

Source: Fairbank, in Fairbank and Feuerwerker (1983: XII, 1–2).

REASONS FOR WAR AGAINST JAPAN   **Document 2**

The Chinese court explains its relationship with Korea, including the reasons why it declared war with Japan. This note from the imperial and court records is dated 1 August 1895, the same day as the declaration of war, equivalent to the first day of the seventh month according to the Chinese lunar calendar.

Korea has been a dependency (*fanshu*) of the Great Qing dynasty for over 200 years, with tribute being sent in annually. This is known to everybody, both in China and abroad. In the last decade and more there has been a great deal of disorder (*luan*) within Korea itself, something of great concern to our court. It has several times sent troops to restore order and personnel to reside in its capital city [Seoul] to be able to afford protection at any time.

In the fourth month of this year [according to the lunar calendar], local rebellion again erupted in Korea, which urgently requested Chinese troops to suppress it . . . Without any reason at all Japan also sent troops, and these immediately entered Seoul. Afterwards Japan increased its troop strength to well over 10,000. Not only that, but it has also forced Korea to change its national government . . .

Although Korea is a dependency of China, Japan has set up a treaty with it [without our permission], and has absolutely no justification for its reinforcement of troops, its oppression of Korea and its removal of the legitimate government. International opinion is united in its inability to find any reasonable name for the army Japan now stations in Korea. Japan has not been amenable to reason, has refused encouragement to order that its troops be withdrawn and refused to enter friendly discussions to restore peace.

Source: Da Qing Dezong Jing (Guangxu) huangdi shilu (1964: V, ch. 344, 3061). Translation by Colin Mackerras.

THE YEAR 1900 AND THE RISE OF NATIONALISM   **Document 3**

Mary Clabaugh Wright, a distinguished historian of modern China, sums up the last decade of the Qing dynasty, and comments on the rise of nationalism.

Rarely in history has a single year marked as dramatic a watershed as did 1900 in China. The weakness laid bare by the Allied pillage of Peking [Beijing] in the wake of the Boxer Rebellion finally forced on China a polar choice: national extinction or wholesale transformation not only of a state but of a civilization. Almost overnight Chinese – imperial government, reformers, and revolutionaries – accepted the challenge. Easily three quarters of the foreign non-official observers – journalists, missionaries, businessmen, doctors, teachers – were dumbfounded at the change. Letters flowed home assuring friends and colleagues who had left China only a few years earlier that they simply would not recognize the country today. A few called the changes superficial, but the great majority supported their impression of a vastly altered ambience with specific observations and experiences . . .

The paramount issue that concerned New China – China in the first phase of revolution – was nationalism, a nationalism directed towards action and change in three different, through related spheres. First it called for action not only to halt but to roll back the tide of imperialism. New China meant to reclaim everything imperial China had ever lost to foreign powers, and in some cases to advance beyond the claims of the Ch'ing [Qing] Empire at its height. Although this was of course an 'antiforeign' sentiment, it should be sharply distinguished from the primitive xenophobia to which the reformers and revolutionaries of the time attributed the antiforeign up-risings of the nineteenth century, which culminated in the Boxer Rebellion of 1900.

Nationalism demanded secondly the organization of a modern, centralized nation-state, capable both of forcing back the imperialists and of forwarding the country's new aspirations in political, social, economic, and cultural life. And thirdly, nationalism meant to overthrow the Manchu dynasty. This anti-Manchuism seems to me to have been less important at the time, and far less important retrospectively, than the anti-imperialist and centralizing thrusts of the new nationalism.

Source: Wright (1968: 1, 3–4).

Document 4   THE COURT'S FLIGHT TO XI'AN

The following is a roadside poster concerning the requisitions of labour and provisions which the court's flight to Xi'an and back to Beijing involved.

The foreign troops came to our town,
In flames the houses tumbled.
Indemnities are huge;
We common folk must pay them . . .

Imperial levies weigh heavy now,
Officials grab like hungry wolves.
Who dares stray near the imperial road,
Is fined three thousand silver taels.

And all along and by this road,
Razed are the houses and ancestral tombs.

Source: Translation from Compilation Group for the 'History of Modern China' Series (1976: 117–18).

PREDICTIONS OF THE FUTURE　　　　　　　　　　**Document 5**

The following comes from an American newspaper editorial on the Boxers, and contemporary with them. It casts bleak judgements on the state of China and its immediate future.

The overthrow of the Manchu dynasty and the restoration of pure Chinese Government might save the empire and make the loss of sovereignty a temporary misfortune. This is improbable. The Chinese are doubtless about to lose the right of the free hand in regulating their internal and external affairs. Subjugation will only hasten decay, and in the case of a vast and undeveloped empire in this age of active public conquest and private exploitation, when the drones and the incapables are being driven out of their fallow estates by the busy and eager workers, decay will be arrested not far in the future by dismemberment, partition, and the industrial dominance of the men of the living nations.

Source: The New York Daily Times editorial, quoted from Beals (1901: 152).

CHINA'S NEUTRALITY IN THE RUSSO-JAPANESE WAR　　　　　**Document 6**

The following concerns China's claim to neutrality in the Russo-Japanese War of 1904–5. It was written by Captain W. F. Tyler, the Coast Inspector, and takes a very pro-Chinese view.

From the beginning of the war China has been most anxious to act in a correct manner, as instanced by the promulgation of neutrality rules which if anything err on the side of strictness. If she has failed in some matters it is not surprising – others have done likewise – and she is willing to accept all responsibility for such lapses as may have occurred. It will be shown presently that such lapses are very few . . .

The fact that practically all the military operations have taken place in territory that was nominally Chinese has been used by the Japanese . . . to show that China's neutrality was imperfect, and that the condition of things was, as regards International Law, an anomaly and a contradiction. Such an expression, especially when used as an excuse for a gross violation of neutrality, is incorrect and unfair. A certain condition of affairs existed in Manchuria anterior to the war. This condition was that the Russians were in military occupation of it without the consent of China. At the time when war commenced China was not exercising full sovereign functions in that part. How and why this condition existed has no bearing on the question of her neutral duties. The fact exists that, when war broke out, utterly insurmountable obstacles stood in the way of fully guarding her neutrality there. No law can lay an obligation on a subject which it is impossible for him to carry out.

Source: Quoted from Morse (1971: III, 479–80).

Document 7   PROMOTING NATIONALISM

In the following passage, which comes from 'Xin min shuo' ('On a New People'), dated 1902, Liang Qichao discusses the notion of nationalism. His view, which emphasises the renewal of the people, is somewhat less radical than those put forward by revolutionaries such as Sun Yat-sen.

Since the sixteenth century, some 300 years ago, the reason why Europe developed and the world progressed was because of the impetus created by widespread nationalism. What is this thing called nationalism? It means that, no matter where you are, people of the same race, the same language, the same religion and the same customs regard each other as relations, work towards independence and autonomy, and organize a better government to work for the public good and to oppose the onslaughts of other nations. When this idea had developed to an extreme at the end of the nineteenth century, it went further and became national imperialism over the last twenty or thirty years. What does national imperialism mean? It means that the power of a nation's citizens has developed domestically to the stage where it cannot help but press outside, so that they industriously try to extend their powers to other regions. The ways of doing this are through military power, commerce, industry or religion, but they use a co-ordinated policy for guidance and protection . . .

 Now on the eastern continent there is located the largest of countries with the most fertile of territory, but the most corrupt of governments, and the most disorganized and weakest of peoples. No sooner had those races [from

Europe] found out about our internal condition than they got their so-called national imperialism moving, just as swarms of ants attach themselves to what is rank and foul and as ten thousand arrows focus on a target . . .

If we want now to oppose the national imperialism of the powers [effectively], rescue China from disaster and save our people, we have no choice but to adopt the policy of pushing our own nationalism. If we are serious about promoting nationalism in China, we have no option but to do it through the renewal of the people.

Source: Liang (1916: I, 3b, 4a–b). Translation by Colin Mackerras.

MANIFESTO OF THE CHINESE UNITED LEAGUE   **Document 8**

The Chinese United League, set up in August 1905 with Sun Yat-sen as president, discusses the expulsion of the Manchus and equal land rights in its Manifesto.

1.   Expel the Manchu barbarians.
The Manchus are eastern barbarians from outside the border. During the Ming dynasty they frequently made trouble along the borders. Later they took advantage of many troubles in China to take over the country. They destroyed our China, seized our government, oppressed the Han people and made us their slaves, massacring countless people who would not submit to them. It is now 260 years since our Han people's country was lost. The Manchu government has reached the ultimate in tyranny. It is time to throw off the yoke of that government and bring back our own sovereignty. Those among the Manchus and their armies who repent and surrender will escape punishment. Those who dare to resist will be killed without scruple. Those Han people who have collaborated with the Manchus and betrayed their own Han people will be treated in the same way.

2.   Restore China.
China is the China of the Chinese, and Chinese must take responsibility for the government of China . . .

3.   Establish a republic.
Our present revolution is one of equals, and all will have equal political rights. The president and members of parliament will all be elected by the whole people. We shall enact the Constitution of the Republic of China, which all will observe equally. We shall all strike at anyone who dares to try and revive the monarchy.

4.   Equal land rights.

The prosperity deriving from civilization will be enjoyed equally by the whole people. We should improve social and economic organization, and evaluate all the country's land. Its current value will belong to the original owner. But any value added from social improvement and progress after the revolution will revert to the state to be enjoyed by all the people . . .

Source: Sun (1981: I, 285–6). Translation by Colin Mackerras.

Document 9   ANTI-MANCHU FEELING

Among the most prominent of the Manchus' critics in the last decade of the Qing dynasty was Zou Rong (1885–1905). In 1903 he put out a pamphlet attacking the Manchus as rulers and as people, using language that Zou himself acknowledges as racist, and apparently with pride. This passage makes clear that Zou would prefer the Europeans as rulers to the Manchus. In other words, he is anti-Manchu, not particularly anti-imperialist, though he acknowledges that there are many in China who do not share his views.

Chapter 2

Origins of Revolution

Revolution! Revolution! Why should my 400 million fellowcountrymen embark on revolution today? I first cry out (and I put all I know into it):

Unjust! Unjust! What is most unjust and bitter in China today is to have to bear with the wolvish ambitions of this inferior race of nomads, the brigand Manchus, our rulers. And when we seek to be wealthy and noble, we wag our tails and beg for pity, we kneel thrice and make ninefold kowtows, delighted and intoxicated to find ourselves under them, shameless and unable to come to our senses. Alas, you have no racial feelings, no feelings of independence!

Today, reformers and enthusiasts are for ever crying out to the public: If urgent reforms are not carried out, China will follow in the footsteps of India, Poland [partitioned in 1795 between Prussia, Russia and Austria] and Egypt, and the tragedy of India and Poland will be played out again in our ancient land . . . But I say: Why do you talk like this? How can you speak so shamelessly and senselessly? What sudden madness had seized you to make you talk so? Are you not aware that we have been in the same position as Poland and India for three hundred years – between the legs of the Manchus – and yet you say: *will be.* Why is this so? I will explain it to you, fellowcountrymen. I say that we are already like Poland or India, under the

Manchu scoundrels; and are the Manchu scoundrels not under the [domination of the] English, French, Russians, Americans and others, [also] like Poland and India? If this is so, let us rather be directly a people without a country. Why do I say this? There is a possibility that our country may be destroyed by the English, French and others, who certainly are on a higher level of civilization than ourselves. I do not understand, fellowcountrymen, why you do not like being the slaves of civilized peoples, and yet are glad to be the slaves of these barbarian slaves [the Manchus].

Source: Tsou [Zou] (1968: 65). The Chinese original is included in the book, with its own internal pagination, the present passage being pp. 4–5.

MANIFESTO OF ZHANG XUN   **Document 10**

The following is part of the manifesto that Zhang Xun issued in mid-1917 stating his reasons for restoring the monarchy. This English version was published by the anti-monarchist Peking Gazette *on 3 July 1917.*

Ever since the uprising at Wuchang and the establishment of the republic peace and order have been cast to the winds and good reliable people have been nowhere to be seen. Anarchists have been holding sway while unscrupulous people have been monopolising the power. Robber chiefs are called heroes and dead convicts are worshipped as martyrs. Parliament relied on rebels for support while Cabinet Ministers used biased parties as their protection. Unscrupulous borrowing of foreign money is called finance; and bleeding the people is termed revenue-raising. Oppression of innocent people is considered self-government; and defaming old scholars is considered civilisation. Some spread rumours under the pretext that they are public opinion while others secretly finance foreigners and call it diplomacy. All these are treason practised under the fine name of statesmanship, and corruption under the mask of legislation. They even advocate the abolition of Confucianism and thus call down the wrath of God . . . Compare this with the continuous reign of a monarchy, wherefrom the people may enjoy peace for tens or hundreds of years, the difference is at once seen to be as great as the distance between heaven and earth . . . . Carefully weighing present conditions and the tendency of the people it is preferable to expel party politics and establish a firm monarchy than to invite ruin by adopting the empty name of a Republic.

Source: Quoted from Johnston (1934: 137–8).

Document 11   MANIFESTO OF ALL THE STUDENTS OF BEIJING

The following is a complete copy of the 'Manifesto of All the Students of Beijing', the only printed material distributed by the students at their demonstration of 4 May 1919. Written by Luo Jialun, a student of Peking University at the time, it appears in English translation in Chow Tse-tsung's classic work The May Fourth Movement. *Romanization is changed here into the* pinyin *system, but the translation is otherwise that of Chow Tse-tsung.*

Japan's demand for the possession of Qingdao and other rights in Shandong is now going to be acceded to in the Paris Peace Conference. Her diplomacy has secured a great victory; and ours has led to a great failure. The loss of Shandong means the destruction of the integrity of China's territory. Once the integrity of her territory is destroyed, China will soon be annihilated. Accordingly, we students today are making a demonstration march to the Allied legations, asking the Allies to support justice. We earnestly hope that all agricultural, industrial, commercial, and other groups of the whole nation will rise and hold citizens' meetings to strive to secure our sovereignty in foreign affairs and to get rid of the traitors at home. This is the last chance for China in her life and death struggle. Today we swear two solemn oaths with all our fellow countrymen: (1) China's territory may be conquered, but it cannot be given away; (2) the Chinese people may be massacred, but they will not surrender.

Our country is about to be annihilated. Up, brethren!

Source: Chow (1960: 106–7).

Document 12   *NEW YOUTH'S* ANSWER TO THE TRADITIONALISTS

The main magazine of the period of the May Fourth Movement was Xin qingnian *(New Youth), founded in 1915, which had a very progressive editorial policy. In January 1919, vol. 6, no. 1, it published its 'Benzhi zuian de dabian shu' ('Letter of Refutation of this Magazine's Crimes') which put forward its advocacy of science and democracy. It attacked the very conservative notion of the 'national essence' (guocui), the term that traditionalists had used to refer to that part of the Chinese tradition that must at all costs be upheld. What the article set out to refute is the charge by traditionalists that the magazine was trying to destroy Chinese culture because of its opposition to Confucianism, Confucianist values and traditional arts and thought.*

Looking into the matter of such charges, this periodical pleads not guilty, on the grounds that our committing these towering crimes is only because of our defence of two gentlemen called Mr Demokelaxi (Democracy) and Mr Saiyinsi (Science). As supporters of Mr Democracy, we have no alternative but to oppose Confucianism, the rites, women's chastity, old moral principles and old politics. As supporters of Mr Science we cannot but oppose those old arts and old religion. Because we support both Mr Democracy and Mr Science, we have no choice but to oppose the national essence (*guocui*) and old literature . . .

We now confidently proclaim that only these two gentlemen can save China from all the darkness in its politics, its morality, its academe and its ideology. We may suffer government oppression, social attack and ridicule from defending these two gentlemen, our heads may be severed and our blood flow, but we shall make no apologies for our position.

Source: Quoted in Research Room of the Chinese Communist Party . . . (1958: I, 9). Translation by Colin Mackerras.

JOINT MANIFESTO OF SUN YAT-SEN AND A. A. JOFFE   Document 13

On 26 January 1923, Sun Yat-sen and Soviet emissary Adolphe Joffe issued a joint communique in Shanghai. In English, the communique symbolized strong mutual support and was a milestone in Sun's career.

Dr. Sun is of the opinion that, because of the non-existence of conditions favourable to their successful application in China, it is not possible to carry out either Communism or even the Soviet system in China. M. Joffe agrees entirely with this view; he is further of the opinion that China's most important and most pressing problems are the completion of national unification and the attainment of full national independence. With regard to these great tasks, M. Joffe has assured Dr. Sun of the Russian people's warmest sympathy for China, and of [their] willingness to lend support.

Source: 'Joint Manifesto of Sun Yat-sen and A. A. Joffe', in Brandt, Schwartz and Fairbank (1971: 70).

THE THREE PRINCIPLES OF THE PEOPLE   Document 14

When Sun became the president of the Chinese United League in August 1905 his nationalist concerns had been directed against the Manchus as the rulers of China, not against the foreign powers. By the time he gave his lectures on the three principles of the people in 1924, his emphasis was completely different.

The Three Principles of the People most violently deplored the danger that Western imperialism represented for China. His second lecture on nationalism, given on February 3, 1924, was entirely devoted to a description of the foreign powers' political and economic oppression in China. On February 24, he returned to and developed these same themes in his fourth lecture.

By political oppression Sun meant the amputations perpetrated upon the national territory; and he enumerated all these despoiliations. He reminded his audience of the concessions wrested at the time of the breakup of China in the late 1890's, proceeded to list the losses that had followed both the Sino-Japanese War (1894–95) and the Sino-French War (1884–85), then went back to the seventeenth century and recalled the secession to Russia of the territories situated north of the Amur River . . .

Since the beginning of the twentieth century, the foreign powers had halted these encroachments, for they had realized how difficult it would be to conquer a territory as vast as the Chinese continent and wished to avoid the rivalries that might have developed between them over the division of such a conquest. They had therefore abandoned political oppression and replaced it with economic oppression, which Sun believed to be even more pernicious because it was more difficult to identify . . .

. . . [T]his view of the Chinese situation led Sun to the unassailable conclusion that China was a country under foreign domination . . . In truth, China's status was not superior, but inferior to that of a colony (toward which the metropolis at least assumed certain responsibilities). China was 'a colony of the Powers' and this made the Chinese 'not the slaves of one country but of all.' Sun invented the term 'hypocolony' (*cizhimindi*) for this ultimate degradation.

Source: Bergère (1998: 360–1).

Document 15   THE THREE PRINCIPLES OF THE PEOPLE: NATIONALISM

In a lecture given on 27 January 1924, Sun Yat-sen explains the three principles of the people, and especially nationalism.

What are the three principles of the people? The simplest definition is that they are the principles of saving the country . . . I ask you, is not this China of ours in need of salvation? If that is the case, then let us put our faith in the three principles of the people. This faith will bring about a great power, which can save China . . .

What is nationalism? According to the social customs and conditions in Chinese history, I would say simply that nationalism is the doctrine of the state-nation (*guozu zhuyi*). What Chinese people worship is the family and clan, so China only adheres to the doctrines of family and clan, not to the state-nation. Foreign observers say that Chinese are a sheet of loose sand. Why is this? It's because the people as a whole care about the doctrines of the family and clan, but not the state-nation. For Chinese, the unifying force of family and clan is very great indeed and many have been willing to sacrifice their families and lives to defend the clan . . . But there has never been a case of such a supreme sacrifice for the sake of the country. So the unifying force of the Chinese extends only to the clan, not as far as to the state-nation.

Source: Sun (1981: I, 1–2). Translation by Colin Mackerras.

THE THREE PRINCIPLES OF THE PEOPLE: DEMOCRACY   **Document 16**

In this lecture, given on 9 March 1924, Sun Yat-sen explains the second of his three principles of the people, democracy.

What is democracy (*minquan zhuyi*) [literally the power of the people]? To explain this concept of 'democracy' we have to know what the people is. Any unified and organized group of persons can be called a people. What is power? It is strength and authority and when such strength is applied to the state we call it power (*quan*) . . . Combining the terms 'the people' and 'power' together, we get 'democracy' or the political strength of the people . . . Politics is the management of affairs involving the masses. So the strength that manages affairs involving the masses is the people's power or democracy. If the people manage political affairs, we call that democracy . . .

When we've set up a genuinely republican state, who will be emperor? The people will be emperor, those 400 million Chinese will be emperor. That way we can prevent people from struggle against each other which will reduce the disaster of war in China . . . Our revolutionary party wanted to avoid war, so as soon as we launched the revolution, we advocated a republic, we didn't want any more emperors. Now it is thirteen years since the republic was established but there are still those who want to become the emperor . . . When China underwent successive dynastic changes, those with the greatest military power competed to set themselves up as emperor, while those with less struggled to become princes and marquises. That the average great military man of today does not dare to call himself a prince or petty one to become a marquis shows that we are making progress in historical terms.

Source: Sun (1981: I, 65, 79). Translation by Colin Mackerras.

Document 17   THE THREE PRINCIPLES OF THE PEOPLE: PEOPLE'S LIVELIHOOD

The following is a definition of the third of 'the three principles of the people', namely minsheng zhuyi, *which means literally 'the principle of the people's livelihood'. This comes from a lecture Sun Yat-sen delivered on 3 August 1924.*

Today I give a definition for this term: *minsheng* is the people's livelihood, the subsistence of society, the nation's welfare, the life of the masses. Now I'll use these two characters (*min* and *sheng*) to talk about a major problem abroad in the last century or so, the problem of society. That is to say, the principle of *minsheng* is socialism, also called communism, or the principle of great harmony . . .

The problem of people's livelihood (*minsheng*) has become a rising tide all over the world. But the problem has only emerged in the last century or so. Why is this? Put simply, it is because over the last few decades there have been major advances in the material civilization of every country, industry has developed greatly, and the productive forces of humankind have suddenly increased . . .

No longer can it be said that the material problem is the centre of history. The political, social and economic centres within history all actually boil down to the problem of the people's livelihood (*minsheng*), so the people's livelihood is the centre of social history. First we must study the central problem of the people's livelihood clearly, and only then can we find a way of solving the problems of society.

Source: Sun (1981: I, 157, 176). Translation by Colin Mackerras.

Document 18   CHIANG KAI-SHEK ENDORSES THE THREE PRINCIPLES
OF THE PEOPLE

In the following passage, Chiang Kai-shek gives his strong endorsement to Sun Yat-sen's three principles of the people. The passage comes from Chapter 6 of Chiang's best known work. Entitled China's Destiny (Zhongguo zhi mingyun), *it was published in March 1943 in Chongqing, China's war-time capital.*

In my article 'The System and Practice of the Three Principles of the People', I stated: The reason why we human beings are different from, and higher than, all animals and can continuously develop and make progress, is because we have emotions, laws, discipline and reason, all of them indispensable for maintaining human survival and pushing forward human progress . . .

Nationalist emotion is the noblest of all human emotions. This is because a nation is formed by the forces of nature, so to unite the nation we must depend on the natural emotions of humankind. As for the principle of democracy, the finest of legal human organizations is the politics of the whole people, which is the politics of democracy. To lay down rules for the duties and privileges of each nation depends entirely upon law and discipline, equitably applied by government. As concerns people's livelihood, the most rational pattern is economic equality of the whole people, without oppression or exploitation, with the interests of the great majority harmonized, and able to reach the state of equality without poverty, harmony without isolation, and peace without instability . . . So I say that nationalism is based on emotion, democracy on law, and the principle of the people's livelihood on reason . . . So emotion, reason, and law each has its own proper function, which means that the three principles of the people are more complete, as well as more far-reaching and easier to implement, than any other doctrine.

It is obvious from this that in the three principles of the people emotion, reason and law each receives its proper emphasis and has its proper place. There are some scholars who argue that China's political philosophy lays stress on rule by propriety or rule by man, but opposes rule by law. This is a misunderstanding. We can see that rule by law has a very important place and function in the three principles of the people.

Source: Chiang (1984: I, 174). Translation by Colin Mackerras.

PLANS FOR RECONSTRUCTION   **Document 19**

The following comes from an account of the platform of the Nationalist Party published in the premier issue of an English-language government-sponsored year book. In it the chapter author (Tsui Wei-wu) discusses the planned progress of government in China.

5. The order of reconstruction is divided into three periods, namely:
    (a) Period of Military Operations;
    (b) Period of Political Tutelage;
    (c) Period of Constitutional Government.

6. During the period of military occupation the entire country should be subject to military rule. To hasten the unification of the country, the government should employ military force to conquer all opposition in the

country and propagate the principles of the Party so that the people may be enlightened.

7.   The period of political tutelage in a province should begin and military rule should cease as soon as order within the province is completely restored.

8.   During the period of political tutelage the government should dispatch trained officers, who have passed the examinations, to the different districts to assist the people in making preparations for local self-government. The attainment of local self-government depends on the completion of the census, the survey of the district, the organization of an efficient police force, and the construction of roads throughout the district. Moreover, the people of the district must be able to fulfil their duties as citizens by exercising the four rights mentioned above [of election, recall, initiative, and referendum], and must pledge themselves to carry out the principles of the revolution before they are entitled to elect the officer of a *hsien* [*xian*, county] for the administration of its affairs and representatives of the *hsien* for the formulation of its laws. By that time, the *hsien* will then be considered as fully self-governing.

9.   The citizens of a full self-governing *hsien* have the right of direct voting for the election of officers, the right of recall, the right of initiating laws, and the right of direct referendum.

10.   At the beginning of self-government it is imperative that a declaration be made of the value of privately owned land of the district, the procedure being to require the owners to make their own declaration at the local administration that the tax will be imposed according to the declared value, but the local government is entitled at any time to purchase the property at the declared value.

Source: Kwei (1935–6: I, 139–40).

———————◀◉▶———————

Document 20   THE NANJING DECADE

A distinguished historian of the period, Lloyd Eastman, gives his assessment of the Nanjing decade.

The Nationalists were granted only ten years from the establishment of their government in Nanking [Nanjing] until the nation was engulfed in a long and devastating war. Ten years was too brief a time to establish a completely new national administration and to turn back the tide of political disintegration and national humiliation that for a century and a half had assailed the nation. Even if conditions had been ideal, the new government could have done little more than initiate political, social and economic reforms.

Despite the adverse conditions afflicting the nation, there had been progress during the decade. By mid-1937, the central government was seemingly ensconced in power, so that there was greater political stability than at any time since 1915. The economy was on the upturn; the government was pushing ahead with various transportation and industrial schemes; the currency was more unified than ever before. Many observers, both Chinese and foreign, believed that the Nationalists had in just ten years reversed the tide of disintegration . . .

The conditions that had generated this swelling optimism, however, were of such recent vintage – appearing less than a year before the war began – that it would be folly for a historian to insist dogmatically that these conditions necessarily portended long-term success and stability for the regime. The improved economic situation, for example, was directly related to the vagaries of China's weather and to the uncertainties inherent in the inflationary trend set off by the creation of a managed currency. The political and military unity of the nation was also extremely fragile, as would become grievously apparent later in the war years. And the popularity of Chiang Kai-shek was attributable to his avowed determination to resist the Japanese rather than to any fundamental reforms in the regime itself.

The new mood of the nation, in other words, had been generated largely by superficial and possibly transient phenomena. Peering beneath those surface features, one discerns that the regime continued to be, even at the end of the Nanking decade, a clumsy and uncertain instrument of national renewal. The civil bureaucracy remained inefficient and corrupt. Government offices were filled with nepotistic appointees who had few if any qualifications for office, but filled the government bureaus with superfluous and self-serving personnel.

Source: Eastman (1974: 48–9).

POPULATION FIGURES   **Document 21**

Chinese statistics for China's overall population in selected years

Year	Total population	Source (all Chinese government)
1912	405,810,967	Minister of the Interior
1928	441,849,148	Minister of the Interior
1933	444,436,537	Bureau of Statistics
1936	479,084,651	Minister of the Interior
1944	464,924,589	Bureau of Statistics

Source: Sun Pen-wen, in Kwei (1944–5: VII, 73).

Chinese statistics for China's overall sex ratios in selected years

Year	Sex ratio
c. 1910	121.6
c. 1931	120.13
1938	119.4
1943	115.6

Source: Kwei (1935–6: I, 121; 1944–5: VII, 73).

Document 22   AN EARLY APPEAL FROM MAO

This extract comes from one of Mao Zedong's earliest articles, written in the summer of 1919. It appeared in July and August that year in three consecutive issues of a weekly called Xiangjiang pinglun (The Xiang River Review), *which Mao established in his native province of Hunan, south-central China.*

Gentlemen! We are peasants, and so we want to establish a union with others who cultivate the land as we do, in order to promote the various interests of us tillers of the soil. It is only we ourselves who can pursue the interests of us tillers of the soil; others who do not cultivate the soil have interests different from ours, and can certainly not help us to seek our interests . . .

Gentlemen! We are workers. We wish to form a union with others who work like ourselves, in order to promote the various interests of us workers. We cannot fail to seek a solution to such problems concerning us workers as the level of our wages, the length of the working day, the equal or unequal sharing of dividends, or the progress of amusement facilities. We cannot but establish a union with those like ourselves to seek clear and effective solutions to each of these problems.

Source: Mao (1972: 80). Translation by Stuart Schram.

Document 23   PEASANT REVOLUTION

Mao Zedong discusses the idea of peasant revolution in a report he wrote in March 1927 of the peasant movement in Hunan.

The present upsurge of the peasant movement is a colossal event. In a very short time, in China's central, southern and northern provinces, several hundred million peasants will rise like a mighty storm, like a hurricane, a force so swift and violent that no power, however great, will be able to hold it back. They will smash all the trammels that bind them and rush forward along the road to liberation. They will sweep all the imperialists, warlords, corrupt officials, local tyrants and evil gentry into their graves. Every revolutionary party and every revolutionary comrade will be put to the test, to be accepted or rejected as they decide. There are three alternatives. To march at their head and lead them? To trail behind them, gesticulating and criticizing? Or to stand in their way and oppose them? Every Chinese is free to choose, but events will force you to make the choice quickly . . .

The main targets of attack by the peasants are the local tyrants, the evil gentry and the lawless landlords, but in passing they also hit out against patriarchal ideas and institutions, against the corrupt officials in the cities and against bad practices and customs in the rural areas. In force and momentum the attack is tempestuous; those who bow before it survive and those who resist perish. As a result, the privileges which the feudal landlords enjoyed for thousands of years are being shattered to pieces. Every bit of the dignity and prestige built up by the landlords is being swept into the dust. With the collapse of the power of the landlords, the peasant associations have now become the sole organs of authority and the popular slogan 'All power to the peasant associations' has become a reality. Even trifles such as a quarrel between husband and wife are brought to the peasant association. Nothing can be settled unless someone from the peasant association is present. The association actually dictates all rural affairs, and, quite literally, 'whatever it says, goes'.

Source: Mao (1965: I, 23–4, 25).

MAO COMMENTS ON THE LONG MARCH   **Document 24**

On 27 December 1935, just after arriving in northern Shaanxi at the end of the Long March, Mao Zedong gave a report to a CCP conference advocating a renewal of the united front, provided it brought about resistance to Japan. In the report he commented glowingly on the Long March.

Speaking of the Long March, one may ask, 'What is its significance?' We answer that the Long March is the first of its kind in the annals of history, that it is a manifesto, a propaganda force, a seeding machine . . . Let us ask, has history ever known a long march to equal ours? No, never. The Long March is a manifesto. It has proclaimed to the world that the Red Army is an army of heroes, while the imperialists and their running dogs, Chiang

Kai-shek and his like, are impotent. It has proclaimed their utter failure to encircle, pursue, obstruct and intercept us. The Long March is also a propaganda force. It has announced to some 200 million people in eleven provinces that the road of the Red Army is their only road to liberation. Without the Long March, how could the broad masses have learned so quickly about the existence of the great truth which the Red Army embodies? The Long March is also a seeding-machine. In the eleven provinces it has sown many seeds which will sprout, leaf, blossom, and bear fruit, and will yield a harvest in the future. In a word, the Long March has ended with a victory for us and defeat for the enemy. Who brought the Long March to victory? The Communist Party. Without the Communist Party, a march of this kind would have been inconceivable.

Source: Mao (1965: I, 160).

Document 25   HIERARCHY WITHIN THE CCP

In October 1938, in the early stages of the War Against Japan, Mao specified his attitude towards discipline and hierarchy within the CCP.

We must affirm anew the discipline of the Party, namely:

(1)   The individual is subordinate to the organization;
(2)   the minority is subordinate to the majority;
(3)   the lower level is subordinate to the higher level; and
(4)   the entire membership is subordinate to the Central Committee.

Whoever violates these articles of discipline disrupts Party unity.

Source: Mao (1965: II, 203–4).

Document 26   SIGNIFICANCE OF THE WAR AGAINST JAPAN

A contemporary scholar sums up the significance of the War Against Japan for Chinese history.

Viewed in terms of the postwar consequences for China, the significance of the Sino-Japanese War of 1937–45 can scarcely be exaggerated. If not for the Sino-Japanese War, it is doubtful whether the Chinese Communist party would ever have come to power. The war provided an ideal environment for exponential growth enabling the Chinese Communist movement to become for the first time in its history a serious contender for national power. At the same time, the war fatally sapped the energies of the Chinese Nationalist government, whose defeat in the civil war of 1946–49 cannot be explained without reference to the antecedent experience of the Sino-Japanese War. And if this were not enough . . . the war itself and its aftermath facilitated a major transformation of the international system in ways that continue to affect us all.

Source: Levine, in Hsiung and Levine (1992: xvii–xviii).

THE NANJING MASSACRE   **Document 27**

This and the following document contain official judgements on the behaviour of the Japanese at the time of the Nanjing Massacre.

The continued killing of prisoners of war and non-combatants by the accused is a breach of the Hague Convention concerning the Customs of War on Land and the wartime treatment of prisoners of war. It constitutes both a war crime and a crime against humanity. In the case of Iwa and Noda, the killing of civilians was a demonstration of military prowess, and this prowess was tested by means of a competition; killing as recreation. Nothing ever could have been more cruel and vicious, and nothing has been more barbarous.

Source: The Verdict of the International Military Tribunal for the Far East on senior officers Iwa Noda and Toshiaki Mukai, 18 December 1947, quoted in Xu (1995: 216).

VERDICT OF THE INTERNATIONAL MILITARY TRIBUNAL   **Document 28**

Matsui retired from service in 1935, resuming active service in 1937 as commander of the Japanese armed forces in Shanghai. Subsequently, he was appointed Commander-in-Chief of the Japanese forces in central China, including forces in Shanghai and of the Tenth Army. It was these forces that he led in the capturing of Nanjing on December 12, 1937 . . . In these six or seven weeks [following the capture], thousands of women were raped, over 100,000 people were killed, and innumerable properties were looted and burnt. When these horrible emergencies reach the climax, namely December

17, Matsui entered the city of Nanjing, and remained there for five to seven days . . . The Tribunal holds that there is adequate evidence to prove that Matsui was fully aware of what had happened. However, it would appear he turned a deaf ear to these acts of terror, or deliberately did not take any effective measures to alleviate them . . .

In view of the seriousness of the charge upon which you have been convicted, the International Military Tribunal of the Far East sentences you to death by hanging.

Source: The Verdict of the International Military Tribunal for the Far East on General Iwane Matsui, 12 November 1948, quoted in Xu (1995: 212–14).

Document 29   THE HENAN FAMINE

In their classic book Thunder Out of China, *Theodore. H. White and Annalee Jacoby focus attention on China during the War Against Japan. In the following extract White describes conditions during the great Henan famine of 1942–3. It is based in part on a visit White made to Henan early in 1943 and missionary contacts.*

Letters of the Protestant missionaries recorded the early stages of the crisis, when the trek started in the fall [of 1942]. Mobs of hungry peasants, their women and children with them, had forced their way into wealthy homes and stripped them of anything that could be carried off. They had rushed into irrigated grain fields to seize the standing crops. In some cases hunger had burned out the most basic human emotions; two maddened parents had tied six children to trees so they could not follow them as they left in search of food . . .

By spring [1943], when we arrived, the more vigorous, disturbing elements had fled to the west, where there was food. Those who remained were wasting in hopelessness with a minimum of violence. The missionaries now reported something worse – cannibalism. A doctor told us of a woman caught boiling her baby; she was not molested, because she insisted that the child had died before she started to cook it. Another woman had been caught cutting off the legs of her dead husband for meat; this, too, was justified on the ground that the man was already dead. In the mountain districts there were uglier tales of refugees caught on lonely roads and killed for their flesh. How much of this was just gruesome legend and how much truth we could not judge. But we heard the same tales too frequently, in too widely scattered places, to ignore the fact that in Honan [Henan] human beings were eating their own kind.

Honan is a fertile province. Before the war, it supported some 30,000,000 people . . . In 1940 and '41 the crops had been poor, and the normal carry-over disappeared; in 1942 the spring wheat failed for lack of rain . . . by autumn the province was destitute.

Source: White and Jacoby (1946: 171–2).

THE CIVIL WAR   **Document 30**

Lionel Max Chassin was a general in the French Air Force, doing most of the research for his book on the Chinese Civil War while serving as vice chief of staff for National Defence from 1946 to 1949. The French original of the book, entitled La Conquête de la Chine par Mao Tse-tung, *came out originally in France in 1952 and is based on intelligence reports and other material that came from the French intelligence in China to the General Staff for National Defence. In this extract, Chassin assesses Mao's victory over Chiang Kai-shek and argues the basic reasons for it.*

At the outset, Mao's chances of success were very slim. Clearly outclassed in numbers and matériel, he dominated only a small territory; he had no money, no resources, no allies. Worst of all, the masters of Russian communism had abandoned him; they had recognized Chiang Kai-shek, his mortal enemy, as the leader of China, and yielded Manchuria to Nationalist sovereignty. Opposing Mao was a man to whom propaganda had given the stature of a giant, a prospective member of President Roosevelt's world-governing Big Four, the master of more than 350 million people, of war-hardened armies, of enormous stocks of modern military matériel, an ally assured of the total support of the great American republic, which in 1945 was the world's most powerful state. Between these two champions, who could have hesitated in his choice?

Four years later Chiang Kai-shek, the Chinese hero, was to find himself a vanquished refugee on the small island of Formosa [Taiwan], while his adversary set himself up in Peking [Beijing] as the master of 480 million human beings. What happened? What were the causes of an event which means so much in the history of humanity?

The profound lesson of the drama that was the Chinese Civil War is this: Even now, in this era of materialism and mechanization, spirit is always predominant, and it is morale that wins battles . . .

Mao had only to follow a beaten track. His external theme was the eternal theme of xenophobic nationalism, of the struggle against foreign imperialists, who themselves but barely emerged from barbarism, had 'enslaved' the higher civilization that was China. As for internal themes, he cleverly appealed to the instincts of social justice and proprietorship which are so strong in the human heart.

Source: Chassin (1965, 247–9).

Document 31   TROOP MORALE

The American Consul reports on forced conscription from Shanghai during the period of the Civil War in China, 1946–9.

Wretched morale, mistreatment of recruits and attempted desertion are commonly reported. When marching through Shanghai recruits have to be roped together. There have been repeated incidents (two well-confirmed) where groups brought here attempted escape and were machine-gunned by guards with resultant killings. Successful desertions often deplete quotas. In such cases some contingent commanders have forcibly seized local coolies to replace deserters.

Source: US Department of State, *Foreign Relations of the United States: China* (1947: 259), quoted in Gittings (1974: 130).

Document 32   THE MOOD OF THE PEOPLE

In a piece written at the end of 1948, the distinguished commentator on China A. Doak Barnett describes his impressions of the collapse of public morale in the southern Chinese provinces of Jiangsu, Zhejiang, Jiangxi, Hunan and Guangdong.

Political demoralization in these areas is almost universal, and morale is incredibly low. Almost no spirit of resistance against the Communists re-mains, and faith in the Central Government seems to have vanished. I talked with people of many sorts – businessmen, educators, rickshaw coolies, civil servants, technicians, merchants. All were psychologically prepared for a basic shift of political control and a change of regime.

This low moral stems from numerous factors: the difficulty of ordinary living, a longing for peace and stability, and a growing mistrust of the Central Government, as well as the ominous reports from fighting fronts. Remarks such as 'This can't go on' or 'Any change will be for the better' are accom-panied by solemn head-shaking and dour expressions. The people with whom I talked face the future, and the prospect of a Communist-dominated government, with emotions that mix resignation, relief, and apprehension in varying degrees.

The 'mood of the people' is an intangible thing that cannot be described in neat formulas or measurable terms. In China, the difficulty of defining the political mood is magnified by the scarcity of media of public expression. Whatever its validity elsewhere, the concept of 'public opinion' is not generally applicable in China because the majority of the population is politically inarticulate. Furthermore, millions of people without access to reliable information have no clear-cut opinions about national political events. They react emotionally to such stimuli as grapevine rumors, incomplete news, distorted reports – and the local price of rice. They feel, rather than understand, political trends. The people I met between Shanghai and Canton [Guangzhou] feel that the time is ripe for a major political change in China. Even those who fear change seem to accept its inevitability with helpless resignation.

Source: Barnett (1963: 97).

CHOOSING A MARRIAGE PARTNER   **Document 33**

The author of this play, Hu Shi, was a liberal thinker and literary figure of the May Fourth Period. The play Zhongsheng dashi (The Greatest Event in Her Life) *was written in 1919 and concerns a young woman's wish to determine her own spouse.*

Yamei:	But you agreed with father you wouldn't go to a fortune teller again.
Mrs Tian:	Yes, I know, I know, but this time I just had to ask a fortune-teller. I got him to come over for a horoscope check on you and Mr Chen.
Yamei:	Oh! Oh!
Mrs Tian:	You must realize that this is the biggest event in your life. You're my only child and I can't just let you marry anybody when you're not compatible with him.
Yamei:	Who says we're not compatible? We've been friends for many years. Of course we're compatible.
Mrs Tian:	You certainly are not. The fortune-teller says you're not compatible.
Yamei:	What would he know about it?
Mrs Tian:	It's not just the fortune-teller. Bodhisattva Guanyin says so, too.

Yamei: What? You mean to say you went to ask Guanyin? Dad's going to have something to say about that when he finds out.

Mrs Tian: I know he's against me over this. He's always against me no matter what I do. But we older people just have to decide such a big event as your marriage. No matter how careful we may be, it's impossible to guarantee we won't make a mistake. But the Bodhisattva will never deceive. And when both the Bodhisattva and fortune-teller say the same thing you really can believe it. [*She stands up, walks over to the desk, and opens a drawer*] Read Guanyin's verse yourself.

Yamei: No, I won't!

Mrs Tian: [*Forced to close the drawer*] Darling, don't be so stubborn. I do like that Mr Chen very much. He looks to me like a very dependable person. You've known him all these years since you met over in Japan, and you say you really know just what kind of man he is. But you're still young and inexperienced, and you could easily be wrong. Even we people in our fifties and sixties don't always dare to trust our own judgement. It was because I didn't dare trust myself that I consulted Bodhisattva Guanyin and the fortune-teller. Guanyin said it wouldn't work out, and the fortune-teller said just the same. Can they really both be wrong? The fortune-teller said that the calculations for your birth dates were the very worst ones in the book of horoscopes. It goes something like, 'If pig and monkey get together, they can only finish badly'. The year and hour you and he were born –

Yamei: Please, mother, enough. I don't want to hear any more. [*She weeps, with both hands over her face*] I hate hearing you talk like this! I know Dad will take a different view from you. I'm sure he will.

Mrs Tian: I don't care what view he takes. No daughter of mine will marry anybody without my agreement.

Source: Hu (1919), in *Zhongguo xin wenxue daxi* (*Compendium of New Chinese Literature*) (IX, 3860–1). Translation by Colin Mackerras.

Document 34   THE CHINESE FAMILY SYSTEM

Lin Yutang (1895–1976), who was at the forefront of advocating Chinese culture and Nationalist China to the West, gives a patriotic comment on the Chinese family system.

The best modern educated Chinese still cannot understand why Western women should organize a 'Society for the Prevention of Cruelty to Animals'. Why bother about the dogs, and why do they not stay at home and nurse their babies? We decide that these women have no children and therefore have nothing better to do, which is probably often true. The conflict is between the family mind and the social mind. If one scratches deep enough, one always finds the family mind at work.

For the family system is the root of Chinese society, from which all Chinese social characteristics derive. The family system and the village system, which is the family raised to a higher exponent, account for all there is to explain in the Chinese social life. Face, favor, privilege, gratitude, courtesy, official corruption, public institutions, the school, the guild, philanthropy, hospitality, justice, and finally the whole government of China – all spring from the family and village system, all borrow from it their peculiar tenor and complexion, and all find in it enlightening explanations for their peculiar characteristics. For from the family system there arises the family mind, and from the family mind there arise certain laws of social behavior.

Source: Lin (1935: 175–6).

CHRISTIANITY AND THE STATUS OF WOMEN   **Document 35**

Chiang Kai-shek's wife, Song Meiling, puts forward her views on Christianity and women in a message she sent to the National Christian Council of China on 6 May 1937.

Christianity has been correctly styled as materialistic, because in Christian lands have developed most of the modern scientific inventions which today go to make life longer and more comfortable. Other nations, such as ancient Greece, have given us the elements of physical science, but only in Christian countries have these sciences fully developed and become the common possession of all. In China we are rapidly introducing these modern ways of living to our people, and they are accepting them without question. The Apostle Paul dignified the whole physical life of man when he said: 'Know ye not that your bodies are the temple of the Holy Spirit . . . ?' A more comfortable physical life is desirable for all, and not merely for the privileged few. Surely it is one of the responsibilities of the followers of Christ to see that 'New Life' is put within the reach of all.

The status of women has been raised wherever the Christian faith has become known. Not so long ago, mission schools in China had to offer girls free tuition and spending money to induce them to accept a modern education. It is to the lasting credit of the missionaries that they used every means to get girls to study. Now these trained women are at the heart of many of the movements working to improve the living conditions and the status of their sisters throughout the provinces. Their faith is already in action. Let us carry our co-operative program, between New Life and the churches, for the improvement of the life of women and children, into every village and hamlet throughout the land. The Christian Church throughout the world is rich in finances and in consecrated enthusiastic youth. Let us concentrate some of these resources upon the great need of our day.

Source: Chiang (1940: 80).

Document 36   TWO VERY DIFFERENT YOUNG WOMEN

Ba Jin's Family (Jia) *was completed in 1931 and is among the most famous, and best, novels of the Republican period. This extract speaks eloquently of the different kinds of women in a well-off family of the time.*

'Mingfeng, Mingfeng!' Juehui's [step]mother was calling from the main building.

'Let me go, madam is calling me,' Mingfeng said in a worried and low voice. 'Madam will be angry with me if I'm late.'

'What does that matter?' Juehui said, smiling. 'Just tell her there was something I asked you to do.'

'Madam won't believe me. If I annoy her, she'll carry on at me dreadfully after the guests go.' Her voice was very low, and nobody in the room could hear but Juehui.

Just then another girl's voice rang out, Juehui's sister Shuhua. 'Mingfeng, madam wants you to go and fill the water-pipes with tobacco!'

He moved aside, letting Mingfeng run out.

Shuhua went out of the main building; seeing Mingfeng she asked her reproachfully. 'Where have you been? Why don't you answer when you're called?'

'I brought Third Young Master some tea,' Mingfeng answered, hanging her head.

'Bringing him tea shouldn't take so long! You're not a mute. Why didn't you answer when I called?' Though only fourteen, Shuhua scolded the bond-maids quite freely and naturally, just like the adults. 'Hurry up. If madam gets to know about this, you'll get a real scolding.' Shuhua turned back towards the house and Mingfeng followed her silently.

Juehui had heard everything and was deeply hurt, as if struck by a whip. His face suddenly turned red with shame. It was he who had brought these reproaches on the girl. His younger sister's attitude riled him. He had wanted to say something in Mingfeng's defence, but there was something that had held him back. He had stood in the dark silently, watching, as though it had nothing to do with him.

They departed, leaving him alone. A beautiful female face reappeared before his mind's eye, full of expression, subservient, bearing no grudges, making no complaints. Like a large sea, it accepted everything, swallowed everything, but without any sound.

From the house, he heard another female voice, and another girl [his cousin] came before his eyes. This was also a beautiful face. But its expressions were quite different: full of resistance, passion, resolution, as if accepting nothing. These two faces represented two kinds of lifestyles and pointed to two fates. He compared them together, and although he didn't know why, he felt more sympathy for the former, and liked it better, but saw more happiness and brightness in the latter.

Source: Ba Jin (1970: IV, 16–17). Translation by Colin Mackerras.

THE MATERNAL INSTINCT   **Document 37**

Lin Yutang puts forward his views on women, as the War Against Japan breaks out.

Confucius says, 'The young should learn to be filial in the home and respectful in society; they should be conscientious and honest, and love all people and associate with the kindly gentlemen. *If after acting on these precepts, they still have energy left, let them read books.*' [Italics in original.] Apart from the importance of this group life, man expresses and fulfils himself fully and reaches the highest development of his personality only in the harmonious complementing of a suitable member of the other sex.

Woman, who has a deeper biological sense than man, knows this. Subconsciously all Chinese girls dream of the red wedding petticoat and the wedding sedan . . . Nature has endowed women with too powerful a maternal instinct for it to be easily put out of the way by an artificial civilization. I have no doubt that nature conceives of woman chiefly as a mother, even more than as a mate, and has endowed her with mental and moral characteristics which are conducive to her role as mother, and which find their true explanation and unity in the maternal instinct – realism, judgment, patience with details, love of the small and helpless, desire to take care of somebody, strong animal love and hatred, great personal and emotional bias and a generally personal outlook on things. Philosophy, therefore, has gone far astray when it departs from nature's own conception and tries to make women happy without taking into account this maternal instinct which is the dominant trait and central explanation of her entire being. Thus with all uneducated and sanely educated women, the maternal instinct is never suppressed, comes to light in childhood and grows stronger and stronger through adolescence to maturity, while with man, the paternal instinct seldom becomes conscious until after thirty-five, or in any case until he has a son or daughter five years old . . . The world becomes a different world for her when a woman becomes an expectant mother. Thenceforth she has no doubt whatever in her mind as to her mission in life or the purpose of her existence. She is wanted. She is needed. And she functions. I have seen the most pampered and petted only daughter of a rich Chinese family growing to heroic stature and losing sleep for months when her child was ill. In nature's scheme, no such paternal instinct is necessary and none is provided for, for man, like the drake or the gander, has little concern over his offspring otherwise than contributing his part.

Source: Lin (1939: 176–7).

————◄●►————

Document 38   THE STUDENT MOVEMENT AND NATIONALISM

An eminent Western authority on the prewar student movement sums it up in terms of nationalism.

Student political vicissitudes must be understood in terms of the dominant theme of twentieth-century Chinese history – nationalism. The prevalent variety of nationalism was neither traditionalistic nor aggressive, but anti-imperialist. The concepts of nationalism and anti-imperialism were so closely linked in the minds of students that the words are almost synonymous when used in reference to the student movement . . .

The classical conflict between impetuous youth and cautious middle age was especially agonizing in the Chinese milieu. Students found discrepancies between learning and reality unbearable . . . Many who had studied Western political science, philosophy, and economics were met upon returning home (an ordeal which some did their best to avoid) by grandfathers who still smoked opium and fathers who maintained concubines. These tradition-bound elders assumed that their educated progeny would perpetuate a family system that was indefensible in the light of what the students had learned in school. Small wonder that disproportionate numbers of radical young intellectuals came from backward, rural areas. Small wonder that they sought total destruction of the old order and had little enthusiasm for governments that blithely tolerated decadence.

Source: Israel (1966: 184, 185–6).

THE STUDENT MOVEMENT AND OPPOSITION TO JAPAN   **Document 39**

An early PRC view of the relationship between student opposition to Japan and to Chiang Kai-shek's regime in the December Ninth Movement.

Because the traitorous Nationalist Party government headed by Chiang Kai-shek adopted a shameless policy of non-resistance, the Japanese imperialists very quickly took over the northeast [in 1931] . . . With one accord the people of the whole country demanded unity to resist Japan. But traitor Chiang Kai-shek on the one hand went down on his knees to Japan to compromise and surrender, and on the other hand intensified his suppression of domestic progressive forces. With counsel from German and Italian fascist advisers, and with loans and arms from the United States imperialists, he launched unprecedently brutal attacks against the red soviet areas [of China]. In the cities and the villages he arrested and massacred progressives . . . and the splendid young people in their hundreds of thousands staged continuous marches, sacrificing themselves under the bloody hands of Chiang Kai-shek. The Japanese imperialists took advantage of the opportunity to intensify their aggression against China . . . with Japanese tanks and vehicles amok on the main streets of Beiping. One respected and beloved primary school student shouted 'down with Japanese imperialism' at one of these military vehicles, a cruel Japanese military policeman immediately throwing him beneath the wheels, where he was crushed.

Japanese vagrants in north and south China carried out evil peddling activities in poisonous commodities with the aim of corrupting China, and smuggled arms, so that the customs and the nation's industry suffered losses. The Fascist Japanese . . . plotted to satisfy Japanese imperialism's ambitions for an 'East Asia Co-Prosperity Sphere'.

Source: Wang (1951: 48–9). Translation by Colin Mackerras.

Document 40 AIMS OF EDUCATION

This is an extract from the document on education Chiang Kai-shek's National Government promulgated on 26 April 1929.

Education in the Republic of China, according to the Three Principles of the People, should take as its aims: to replenish and enrich the people's life; to foster social existence; to develop the livelihood of the citizens; and to continue the life of the nation. We aspire to national independence and the widespread realisation of the people's rights, and the development of the people's livelihood, in order to promote the Great Harmony on Earth (*datong*) . . .

Opportunities in education for males and females are equal. Education for girls must pay great attention to moulding a sound and healthy morality in them, to preserving the special qualities of motherhood, and also to building up good family life and social life.

Source: Translated by Colin Mackerras. See also Pong and Fung (1985: 155, 173).

Document 41 THE IMPACT OF POPULAR LITERATURE

This is an extract from an article on 'Popular Literature in Relation to the Masses', which Liang Qichao originally published in 1902.

If you wish to reform the citizens of a country, you must first reform the popular literature of the country. To reform ethical standards, you must reform the popular literature; to reform religion, you must reform the popular literature; to reform the political system, you must reform the popular literature; to reform customs, you must reform the popular literature; to reform learning and improving technology, you must reform the popular literature; to reform people's hearts and characters, you must reform the popular literature. Why? Because popular literature wields incredible influence over the ways of the world.

Source: Translated in Fei (1999: 109).

A NEW LITERARY STYLE   **Document 42**

Chen Duxiu was among the leading thinkers of the New Culture Movement. In the famous journal New Youth, *he proposed getting rid of the literary style of classical Chinese and replacing it with a more popular and accessible way of writing.*

(1)   Get rid of the ornate, adulatory aristocratic literature; create a simple, honest and expressive national literature.
(2)   Get rid of the stale, ostentatious literature in the style of classics; create a fresh, sincere and realistic literature.
(3)   Get rid of the obscure and difficult literature of hermit style; create a lucid and popular literature.

Source: Chen Duxiu, 'On the literary revolution', *New Youth*, February 1917; translation from Tang (1993: 4).

LITERATURE AND ART AS PROPAGANDA   **Document 43**

In the forum he held on literature and the arts in May 1942 in Yan'an, Mao Zedong proposed that literature and arts represented particular classes and should function as propaganda for the revolution.

In the world today all culture, all literature and art belong to definite classes and are geared to definite political lines. There is in fact no such thing as art for art's sake, art that stands above classes or art that is detached from or independent of politics. Proletarian literature and art are part of the whole revolutionary cause; they are, as Lenin said, cogs and wheels in the whole revolutionary machine. Therefore, [Chinese Communist] Party work in literature and art occupies a definite and assigned position in Party revolutionary work as a whole and is subordinated to the revolutionary tasks set by the Party in a given revolutionary period . . . Literature and art are subordinate to politics, but in their turn exert a great influence on politics. Revolutionary literature and art are part of the whole revolutionary cause, they are cogs and wheels in it, and though in comparison with certain other and more important parts they may be less significant and less urgent and may occupy a secondary position, nevertheless, they are indispensable cogs and wheels in the whole machine, an indispensable part of the entire revolutionary cause. If we had no literature and art even in the broadest and most ordinary sense, we could not carry on the revolutionary movement and win victory.

Source: Mao (1965: III, 86).

Document 44   MASS ART

At the Yan'an forum of May 1942, Mao put forward very strong views in favour of 'mass art', even though he did not reject the idea of learning from China's or the West's traditions.

We should take over the rich legacy and the good traditions in literature and art that have been handed down from past ages in China and foreign countries, but the aim must still be to serve the masses of the people. Nor do we refuse to utilize the literary and artistic forms of the past, but in our hands these old forms, remoulded and infused with new content, also become something revolutionary in the service of the people.

    Who, then, are the masses of the people? The broadest sections of the people, constituting more than 90 per cent of our total population, are the workers, peasants, soldiers and urban petty bourgeoisie. Therefore, our literature and art are first for the workers, the class that leads the revolution. Secondly, they are for the peasants, the most numerous and most steadfast of our allies in the revolution. Thirdly, they are for the armed workers and peasants, namely, the Eighth Route and New Fourth Armies and the other armed units of the people, which are the main forces of the revolutionary war. Fourthly, they are for the labouring masses of the urban petty bourgeoisie and the petty-bourgeois intellectuals, both of whom are also our allies in the revolution and capable of long-term co-operation with us. These four kinds of people constitute the overwhelming majority of the Chinese nation, the broadest masses of the people.

Source: Mao (1965: III, 76–7).

Document 45   SPOKEN DRAMA

The following extract beautifully summarizes the role of the spoken drama in twentieth-century Chinese literature and its relationship with the traditional theatre. It comes from the 'Introduction' to an anthology of twentieth-century Chinese drama and is written by one of the acknowledged specialists on the subject.

    The twentieth century has been a period of intense activity and innovation in Chinese drama. Experimenting with operatic tradition and building a new 'spoken drama' . . . , dramatists have expanded the esthetic range of Chinese theater and kept the drama at the forefront of social, political, and artistic controversies. Two fundamental considerations should be kept in mind as part of the particular background for this drama. Much of it is derived from Western dramatic literature, which is represented chiefly by plays written by men in their forties and fifties after arduous apprenticeships in well-established European traditions of drama. In China, by contrast, this spoken drama was adopted primarily by younger writers with far less training and fewer theatrical resources at their command. Indeed, for most of the Chinese writers the form of spoken drama itself was an iconoclastic statement, designed to convey broader views for social reform and revolution. Given its inherently public nature and the social views of the writers, spoken drama has been the most assertive form of innovative literature in modern Chinese society . . .

The most immediate form of competition these young writers have confronted has not, then, been the work of their Western inspirations, but rather the highly developed and well-entrenched traditional Chinese theater, the second of our preliminary considerations. The various forms of opera that over the centuries came to form the Chinese theater were still enormously popular at the beginning of this [the twentieth] century and have remained so. They order a wide range of emotions into standard patterns of music . . . They enact stories usually drawn from popular history and legend, illustrating the moral order of traditional society. Numerous formal innovations have repeatedly brought change and variety to the opera, but as of the early decades of this [the twentieth] century far less was being witnessed in the way of new psychological or moral vision.

Source: Gunn, in Gunn (1983: vii).

THE WHITE-HAIRED GIRL: A REVOLUTIONARY OPERA   **Document 46**

The following is an extract from the final scene of the revolutionary opera The White-Haired Girl (Baimao nü). *Xier, the central figure, is raped by Landlord Huang and escapes to the mountains, where she suffers privations so severe that her hair turns white, but eventually revenges Huang when the CCP's Red Army liberates the area where she lives. Mao Zedong saw the opera in Yan'an in April 1945 and pronounced it excellent.*

Chorus: Country folk, comrades, don't cry,
              The old society forced people to become ghosts,
              But the new society changes ghosts into people,
              It's saved our unfortunate good sister . . .
Xier [*sings*]: I lived in a wild cave deep in the mountains,
              I didn't see the sun, I didn't see anybody,
              I ate raw and cold things, and offerings,
              And seemed like neither ghost nor person.

Water may run dry and stones may wear through,
But I would not die,
And have borne bitter suffering till now . . .

Chorus: Today is for us, the masses,
We'll be revenged, we'll be revenged, we'll be revenged!
We demand justice, we demand justice,
We want vengeance for Xier! . . .
You've bowed your head, Landlord Huang!
You're trembling with fear!
You've bowed your head!
You're trembling with fear!
Your feudal ties of a thousand years
We've cut away today!
Your heavy iron chains
We've smashed to smithereens! . . .
For countless generations we've suffered bitterness,
But now we're throwing off oppression
And we're the masters! And we're the masters!

Source: He, Ding and Ma (1964: 22, 27–31). Translation by Colin Mackerras.

Further Reading

This guide to further reading introduces some of the main books in English written on topics relevant to the present work, especially those specifically covered in the chapters dealing with China in the first half of the twentieth century. All the books mentioned here are included in the References, which is why items are given here only by author and date. The books discussed are generally classified according to their topic, although of course there is frequently overlap between topics, so I have classified books according to the category that would seem most obvious or relevant to users.

Although there was already good scholarship and reporting about the first half of the twentieth century carried out at the time, most of the material on which I have relied for the present book has been published since the CCP came to power in 1949. I offer here a very broad summary of the trends in thinking that have affected the main scholarship on China in the first half of the twentieth century.

The CCP's victory exercised a profound impact not only over ideas about contemporary China but over what had happened beforehand. Mainstream scholarship tended to sympathize with pre-1949 regimes, especially China's opposition to Japanese and other colonialism and to communism. Access to Chinese scholarship and libraries about the pre-1949 period was heavily dominated by Taiwan and Hong Kong. Probably the main scholar in the field was the Harvard academic John King Fairbank.

American and other intervention in Vietnam from 1965 to 1975 produced a much more radical stream of scholarship in the West. In general this was more critical of the role of the West and more sympathetic to the record of the Communists than what had come before. It took more interest in subaltern social sectors, such as women, minorities and youth, than had been the case before. This new thinking applied to the past as well as the present.

With the end of the Vietnam War and the beginning of reform in China, scholarship took new directions again. Chinese scholars produced much more about the first half of the twentieth century than had happened before and, though the Taiwan connection remained very strong, it became possible for Westerners to travel in China and to explore libraries there. The views of the CCP about Chinese history remained very strong, but scholars writing in English increasingly tended to challenge the CCP's opinions in almost every area. Feminist viewpoints on history flowered. Many young Chinese who had gone to the West for study remained there, some of them joining the ranks of a new generation of scholars researching their own country, including its history in the first half of the twentieth century.

PRIMARY SOURCES

Two very valuable sets of yearbooks are Woodhead and Bell (1912–39) and Kwei (1935–6 to 1944–5). The survey by the Chinese Ministry of Information (1944) is not a yearbook, but contains similar detailed and valuable information.

Collections of the works of leading figures in translation include Sun (1927), Chiang (1947), Mao (1965–77) and Chiang (1940). Tsou (1968) offers the original Chinese as well as translation. Though its author was not nearly as important as Sun Yat-sen, Chiang Kai-shek, Mao Zedong or Song Meiling, this item still has considerable interest.

There are several collections of documents on the history of the CCP. They include Wilbur (1956), Brandt, Schwartz and Fairbank (1971) and Saich (1996), the last of which contains numerous documents referring to the period from the birth of the CCP in 1920 to the eve of its victory in 1949.

SECONDARY SOURCES

Almost all works in English fall into the category of secondary sources, since primary sources are overwhelmingly in Chinese.

Reference works

The main reference work in English referring only to China in the Republican era is Boorman (1967–79). Clark and Klein (1971) covers only those figures relevant to Chinese communism, and continues down to 1965. A chronology covering the whole of the first half of the twentieth century and also several decades both before and after that time is Mackerras (1982).

General histories, with focus on the first half of the twentieth century or periods within it

There are a number of good general histories of modern China that focus on the first half of the twentieth century, though all have other major coverage as well. The two best known are Spence (1990) and Hsü (1995), both dealing with 'modern China'. Both are excellent in their own way, though Spence is easier to read for the greater emphasis he places on human stories. Gray (1990) puts the focus on rebellion and revolution from the 1800s through to the 1980s. About half of McAleavy (1967) deals with the first half of the twentieth century, and it is a highly competent work, though slightly dated now. Bailey (2001), Moise (1994) and Phillips (1996) are succinct and highly professional treatments. Each deals with slightly different periods, all devoting about half their coverage (slightly less in the case of Moise) to the first half of the twentieth century or years within it. An excellent study, focusing full attention on the Republic of China, including Taiwan since 1949, is Lary (2007).

Wright (1968) is a highly original study of the first dozen or so years of the twentieth century. The most important work about Republican China is Fairbank and Feuerwerker (1983 and 1986), two volumes of the authoritative and multi-volumed *The Cambridge History of China*. Sheridan (1975) is also a major study covering the whole Republican period, summarizing it as 'China in disintegration'. Bianco (1971) focuses its analysis on revolution, covering the period 1915–49. Excellent studies to focus on the Nationalist Revolution of the 1920s include Waldron (1995) and the highly interpretative and analytical Fitzgerald (1996), though the most thorough is Wilbur (1984).

A pre-eminent scholar of the period when Chiang Kai-shek ruled China is Lloyd Eastman. His study of the Nanjing decade (Eastman, 1974) remains the best general treatment of the years 1927–37, while Eastman (1984) covers the period down to Chiang's fall in 1949. Eastman et al. (1991) is a superb collection of essays covering the whole period from 1927 to 1949, previously published as part of volume XXIII of *The Cambridge History of China*. A journalistic but still classic study of the period of the War Against Japan, full of first-hand reporting of conditions in China at the time, is White and Jacoby (1946). There are several very good studies just of the war period, including Boyle (1972), Ch'i (1982) and Hsiung and Levine (1992), the last item covering various aspects of war history, such as diplomacy, the Communist movement, the military dimension, the economy, legal reform, science and literature and the arts. On the postwar years 1945 to 1949, Chassin (1965), originally published in 1952, takes much of its most interesting information from French intelligence, while Melby (1969) presents detailed day-by-day records from somebody closely involved in what he is describing. The best study from a general political point of view is still Pepper (1978). Barnett (1963) takes a close, first-hand and fascinating look at conditions in China in the last years of the Civil War.

Biography

An important category for any guide to further reading is biography. The two figures of the period to receive the most biographical attention are Sun Yat-sen and Mao Zedong. Each has been the subject of an officially sponsored myth, which Western scholarship has undermined or even demolished. However, Sun has generally received kinder treatment than Mao, who has been fully demonized in at least one biography.

Full-length biographies of Sun Yat-sen include Martin (1944), a very posit-ive treatment indeed that attributes 'strange vigour' to its subject; Schiffrin (1968 and 1980), the former work dealing only with his earlier career, the latter summing him up as a 'reluctant revolutionary'; and Wilbur (1976), which describes him as a 'frustrated patriot'. Apart from Martin's biography, these works have tended to demytholigize Sun's career and ideas, while still recognizing his historical role. Bergère (1998), originally published in French in 1994, is a good summation of Sun's career and historical role, avoiding both the hagiographical style found among many Chinese writers and the condescension typical of Western scholarship.

In the case of Mao, demythologizing has gone further than with Sun. An early biography was Schram (1966), a very scholarly and thorough treatment that gives Mao credit for patriotism and some sincerity. A highly hagio-graphic account that is almost entirely about the period down to 1949 is Han (1972). Wilson (1977) came out just after Mao's death. The treatment here is topical, considering Mao as a philosopher, Marxist, political leader, soldier, patriot, statesman and so on. It is generally very positive about Mao, its preface beginning by calling Mao 'a world figure of more than ordinary proportions' who presided over 'the international redemption and internal modernization' of the Chinese people (Wilson, 1977: vii).

Three leading, more recent, biographies (Terrill, 1995; Short, 1999; and Chang and Halliday, 2005) devote about half or more of their total space to the pre-1949 period. Terrill gives attention to Mao's failings, but still describes him as a Titan (1995: 443); the 1995 edition adds a postscript that makes it more critical of Mao than the initial 1980 version, but has essen-tially the same judgements. Short is comprehensive and well documented. Like Terrill, it reflects the trend of more critical thinking about Mao and his influence, but remains balanced and highly thoughtful, probably the best of the biographies of Mao. Chang and Halliday claim to tell an 'unknown story' based in part on Russian archives and extensive interviewing. Bitterly critical of Mao, they portray him as a selfish and power-hungry monster with virtually no redeeming features.

Among numerous other biographical studies concerning the first half of the twentieth century are Thompson and Macklin (2004), about the Australian George Ernest Morrison, whose life was closely tied up with China in the late nineteenth and early decades of the twentieth centuries; Grieder (1970), which deals with Hu Shi and liberalism in China from 1917 to 1937; and Behr (1987), about China's last emperor Puyi. Three biographies of individual warlords are McCormack (1977) about Zhang Zuolin; Sheridan (1966) about Feng Yuxiang; and Wou (1978) about Wu Peifu. The best-selling book Chang (1991) is possibly the most widely read of all English-language books about twentieth-century China. Giving major focus to the first half of the century, as well as to the first twenty years or so of the second half, it deals with the author's grandmother, parents, as well as herself.

Among autobiographical accounts, a large-scale one is that by Zhang Guotao (Chang, 1971 and 1972), who was a major figure in the early history of the CCP (see Chapter 8). His influence declined rapidly after he quarrelled with Mao Zedong in the mid-1930s and he left Yan'an in disgust in 1938.

Politics and government

Apart from the general works discussed above there is also a literature on specific themes in Chinese politics and government in the first half of the twentieth century. Young (1977) discusses the presidency of Yuan Shikai. Several works deal with warlords and warlord politics. These include Pye (1971), Ch'i (1976), McCord (1993) and Bonavia (1995). Among works about the political process are Ch'ien (1950) and Zhao (1996). Pong and Fung (1985) cover various political and social themes.

The economy

Two works in a still very small literature dealing with general economic trends in the first half of the twentieth century are Wright (1992) and Feuerwerker (1977). A pioneering study of land and land utilization is Buck (1964). Wright (1984) handles the coal mining industry to the eve of the War Against Japan. Specific aspects of the economy are handled in Porter (1994) and Pomeranz (1993).

The May Fourth and student movements

The classic work on the May Fourth Movement remains Chow (1960). Others include Chen (1971), which deals with Shanghai, and Schwarcz (1986), with a focus on intellectuals, the latter being a book that uses the term 'Chinese Enlightenment' to refer to the May Fourth Movement. The major study of the May Thirtieth Movement of 1925 is Rigby (1980), while two general studies of student nationalism are Israel (1966) and Li (1994).

Communism and the Communist Party to 1949

There is now a substantial and growing literature on communism and the CCP's revolution before 1949. Major general histories of the CCP with primary focus on the period to 1949 include Schwartz (1951), Guillermaz (1972), Harrison (1973) and Saich and van de Ven (1995). Schwartz, analyses the individual pre-1949 leaders and their strategy and concludes that the successful Maoist strategy was based essentially on a Leninist political party, and faith in certain Marxist-Leninist tenets imposed 'onto a purely peasant mass base' (1951: 189). Saich and van de Ven bring together many of the foremost authorities on the rise of communism in China who gathered at a conference in the Netherlands in 1990. Contributions rely largely on materials that had become public since the beginnings of the reform period in China in 1978. Among numerous other points they emphasize regional variations in the operation of the CCP, casting doubt on the degree of Leninist control that had been a major part of conventional wisdom to that time.

By far the most important study on the origins of Marxism in China is Dirlik (1989). Books on early Marxist thinkers include Meisner (1967) about Li Dazhao; Feigon (1983) about Chen Duxiu; and Knight (1996) about Li Da. On the early years of the CCP and Marxist thinking important works are Saich (1991) and van de Ven (1991). A highly significant account of the years 1927 to 1935, when Mao was 'in opposition' to Moscow's line on China, is Rue (1966). The two main studies of the Long March are Wilson (1971), which puts over a fairly positive view of the event, and Sun (2006), which is much more critical, especially of Mao's role.

Snow (1972) is still an important classic by a journalist very sympathetic to the CCP, who in 1936 visited the CCP areas of northern Shaanxi and interviewed Mao Zedong. It has a great deal to say about the early career of Mao Zedong and conditions in the CCP-controlled areas on the eve of the

War Against Japan. Among works about Mao Zedong's ideas, with substantial focus on the period before 1949 and especially the Yan'an period, a pioneering work is Schram (1969), which consists of a long introduction followed by chapters on particular aspects of Mao's political thought. The much later Knight (2007) departs from several of major aspects of conventional wisdom about Mao's ideas, as well as from several of Schram's main interpretations.

The years when Mao Zedong was in Yan'an (1936–47) have attracted a great deal of scholarly attention, because of their implications for the rise of Mao to a position strong enough that he could take over the whole country. Johnson (1962) was particularly influential for his theory that nationalism was the core factor behind the eventual victory of the CCP. Through research on CCP activities in particular parts of China, several authors have produced books that put forward perspectives alternative or complementary to Johnson's. Particularly important examples are Selden (1971 and 1995), but there are others, such as Wou (1994), Chen (1986), Feng and Goodman (2000) and Keating (1997). There is a brief discussion of the controversy in Chapter 14.

Levine (1987) makes a major contribution to the study of the CCP in the aftermath of the war through examining the situation in the northeast. Two extremely important first-hand studies of the rural revolution not long before the CCP's victory, both very sympathetic to the CCP's cause, are Hinton (1966) and Crook and Crook (1979).

Society, women

The classic general study of Chinese society during the 1920s and 1930s is Lang (1946). Lin (1935 and 1939) offer commentary on Chinese society in more general terms, written from the standpoint of a Chinese aiming to appeal to a Western audience. An admirable examination of the labour movement from the May Fourth Movement until its suppression in 1927 is Chesneaux (1968).

There is a substantial and growing literature on women in the first half of the twentieth century, and it has benefited greatly from the feminist emphasis on women's studies since the 1980s. An early and excellent study is Snow (1967). Siu (1982) examines women's resistance to imperialism in the first half of the twentieth century. Wang (1999) looks at the role of women in the intellectual ferment, centring on the May Fourth Movement, while Gilmartin (1995) studies the mass movements of the 1920s from a similar point of view.

Literature, theatre

Although the first half of the twentieth century is covered to some extent in general works on Chinese literature and theatre, books with a major focus on that period are still quite few. Tang (1993) covers 'modern Chinese literature', 'modern' encompassing the period from 1919 to 1949. McDougall and Louie (1997) divide the material into three periods, 1900–37, 1938–65 and 1966–89, but about half the treatment is about the first half of the twentieth century. This work is useful for its overall analysis of the periods and for its extensive consideration of individual writers. Goldman (1977) is a pioneering work focusing on the May Fourth period. There are several studies of Lu Xun and his work, an excellent example being Lee (1987), as well as of several other writers whose main work was produced in the 1930s.

A work well over half of which covers the general history of theatre in the first half of the twentieth century is Mackerras (1975). For traditional theatre the major study focusing on this period is Goldstein (2007), which deals with the 're-creation of Peking Opera' over the period 1870 to 1937. For the modern theatre, the premier work is still Gunn (1983). An anthology of twentieth-century plays, half of them from the years 1919 to 1949, the work also contains an insightful introduction.

References

Ba Jin, *Ba Jin wenji* (*Collected Works of Ba Jin*), 14 vols, Nan Kwok Publishing Co., Hong Kong, 1970.

Bailey, Paul J., *China in the Twentieth Century*, 2nd edn, Blackwell Publishers, Oxford, 2001.

Barnett, A. Doak, *China on the Eve of Communist Takeover*, Frederick A. Praeger, New York, 1963.

Beals, Rev. Z. Chas., *China and the Boxers; A Short History on the Boxer Outbreak, with Two Chapters on the Sufferings of Missionaries and a Closing One on the Outlook*, Munson, New York, 1901.

Behr, Edward, *The Last Emperor*, Futura Publications, Macdonald & Co., London, 1987.

Bergère, Marie-Claire, *Sun Yat-sen*, trans. Janet Lloyd, Stanford University Press, Stanford, 1998.

Bianco, Lucien, *Origins of the Chinese Revolution, 1915–1949*, trans. Muriel Bell, Stanford University Press, Stanford, 1971.

Bonavia, David, *China's Warlords*, Oxford University Press, Oxford and New York, 1995.

Boorman, Howard L. (ed.), *Biographical Dictionary of Republican China*, 5 vols, Columbia University Press, New York, 1967–79.

Boyle, John H., *China and Japan at War, 1937–1945: The Politics of Collaboration*, Stanford University Press, Stanford, 1972.

Brandt, Conrad, Benjamin Schwartz and John K. Fairbank (eds), *A Documentary History of Chinese Communism*, Harvard University Press, Cambridge, Mass., and Allen & Unwin, London, 1952; Atheneum, New York, 1971.

Buck, John Lossing, *Land Utilization in China: A Study of 16,786 Farms in 168 Localities, and 38,256 Farm Families in Twenty-two Provinces in China, 1929–1933*, University of Nanking, Nanking, 1937; Paragon Book Reprint, New York, 1964.

Chang, Jung, *Wild Swans: Three Daughters of China*, HarperCollins, London, 1991.

Chang, Jung and Jon Halliday, *Mao, The Unknown Story*, Jonathan Cape, London, 2005.

Chang Kuo-t'ao, *The Rise of the Chinese Communist Party, 1921–1927* (vol. I of *Autobiography of Chang Kuo-t'ao*), The University Press of Kansas, Lawrence, Manhattan, Wichita, 1971.

Chang Kuo-t'ao, *The Rise of the Chinese Communist Party, 1928–1938* (vol. II of *Autobiography of Chang Kuo-t'ao*), The University Press of Kansas, Lawrence, Manhattan, Wichita, 1972.

Chassin, Lionel M., *The Communist Conquest of China: A History of the Civil War, 1945–49*, Harvard University Press, Cambridge, Mass., 1965.

Chen, Joseph T., *The May Fourth Movement in Shanghai: The Making of a Social Movement in Modern China*, Brill, Leiden, 1971.

Chen Yung-fa, *Making Revolution: The Communist Movement in Eastern and Central China, 1937–1945*, University of California Press, Berkeley, 1986.

Chesneaux, Jean, *The Chinese Labor Movement, 1919–1927*, trans. H. M. Wright, Stanford University Press, Stanford, 1968.

Ch'i, Hsi-sheng, *Warlord Politics in China, 1916–1928*, Stanford University Press, Stanford, 1976.

Ch'i, Hsi-sheng, *Nationalist China at War: Military Defeats and Political Collapse, 1937–1945*, University of Michigan Press, Ann Arbor, 1982.

Chiang Kai-shek, *China's Destiny and Chinese Economic Theory*, with notes and commentary by Philip Jaffe, Roy Publishers, New York, 1947.

Chiang Kai-shek, *Xian zongtong Jianggong quanji* (*Complete Works of the Late President Jiang*), 3 vols, China Culture University Press, Taibei, 1984.

Chiang, May-ling Soong, *China in Peace and War: Selections from the Writings of May-ling Soong Chiang* (*Madame Chiang Kai-shek*), Kelly & Walsh, Shanghai, 1940.

Ch'ien Tuan-sheng, *The Government and Politics of China*, Harvard University Press, Cambridge, Mass., 1950, reprinted 1961.

Chinese Ministry of Information, *China Handbook 1937–1944: A Comprehensive Survey of Major Developments in China in Seven Years of War*, Chinese Ministry of Information, Chungking, 1944.

Chow Tse-tsung, *The May Fourth Movement: Intellectual Revolution in Modern China*, Harvard University Press, Cambridge, Mass., 1960.

Clark, Anne B. and Donald W. Klein, *Biographic Dictionary of Chinese Communism 1921–1965*, Harvard University Press, Cambridge, Mass., 1971.

Cohen, Paul A., *Discovering History in China: American Historical Writing on the Recent Chinese Past*, Columbia University Press, New York, 1984.

Compilation Group for the 'History of Modern China' Series, *The Yi Ho Tuan Movement of 1900*, Foreign Languages Press, Peking, 1976.

Crook, Isabel and David Crook, *Mass Movement in a Chinese Village, Ten Mile Inn*, Routledge & Kegan Paul, London and Henley, 1979.

Da Qing Dezong Jing (Guangxu) huangdi shilu (*The Veritable Records of Dezong, Emperor Jing (Guangxu) of the Great Qing Dynasty*), (no. 12 in the series *Da Qing lichao shilu* (*The Veritable Records of Successive Reigns of the Great Qing*)), 8 vols, Hualian Press, Taibei, 1964.

Dirlik, Arif, *The Origins of Chinese Communism*, Oxford University Press, New York, 1989.

Eastman, Lloyd, *The Abortive Revolution: China Under Nationalist Rule, 1927–1937*, Harvard University Press, Cambridge, Mass., 1974, reprinted 1990.

Eastman, Lloyd E., *Seeds of Destruction: Nationalist China in War and Revolution, 1937–1949*, Stanford University Press, Stanford, 1984.

Eastman, Lloyd E., Jerome Ch'en, Suzanne Pepper and Lyman P. Van Slyke, *The Nationalist Era in China, 1927–1949*, Cambridge University Press, Cambridge, 1991.

Fairbank, John K. and Albert Feuerwerker (eds), *Republican China, 1912–1949*, Parts I and II, (vols XII and XIII of *The Cambridge History of China*), Cambridge University Press, Cambridge, 1983 and 1986.

Fei, Faye Chunfang (ed. and trans.), *Chinese Theories of Theater and Performance from Confucius to the Present*, University of Michigan Press, Ann Arbor, 1999.

Feigon, Lee, *Chen Duxiu: Founder of the Chinese Communist Party*, Princeton University Press, Princeton, 1983.

Feng Chongyi and David S. G. Goodman (eds), *North China at War: The Social Ecology of Revolution, 1937–1945*, Rowman & Littlefield, Lanham, 2000.

Feuerwerker, Albert, *Economic Trends in the Republic of China 1912–1949*, Center for Chinese Studies, Michigan University, Ann Arbor, 1977.

Fitzgerald, John, *Awakening China: Politics, Culture and Class in the Nationalist Revolution*, Stanford University Press, Stanford, 1996.

Fung, Edmund S. K., *The Diplomacy of Imperial Retreat: Britain's South China Policy, 1924–1931*, Oxford University Press, Hong Kong, 1991.

Gilmartin, Christina Kelley, *Engendering the Chinese Revolution: Radical Women, Communist Politics, and Mass Movements in the 1920s*, University of California Press, Berkeley, 1995.

Gittings, John, *The World and China, 1922–1972*, Eyre Methuen, London, 1974.

Gladney, Dru C., *Muslim Chinese, Ethnic Nationalism in the People's Republic*, published by the Council on East Asian Studies, Harvard University, and distributed by Harvard University Press, Cambridge, Mass., and London, 1991.

Goldman, Merle (ed.), *Modern Chinese Literature in the May Fourth Era*, Harvard University Press, Cambridge, Mass., 1977.

Goldstein, Joshua, *Drama Kings, Players and Publics in the Re-creation of Peking Opera, 1870–1937*, University of California Press, Berkeley, Los Angeles and London, 2007.

Gray, Jack, *Rebellions and Revolutions: China from the 1800s to the 1980s*, Oxford University Press, Oxford, 1990.

Grieder, Jerome B., *Hu Shih and the Chinese Renaissance: Liberalism in the Chinese Revolution, 1917–1937*, Harvard University Press, Cambridge, Mass., 1970.

Guillermaz, Jacques, *A History of the Chinese Communist Party*, trans. Anne Destenay, Methuen, London, and Random House, New York, 1972.

Gunn, Edward M. (ed.), *Twentieth-Century Chinese Drama, An Anthology*, Indiana University Press, Bloomington, 1983.

Han, Suyin, *The Morning Deluge: Mao Tsetung and the Chinese Revolution, 1893–1954*, Little, Brown and Company, Boston, Toronto, 1972.

Harrison, James P., *The Long March to Power: A History of the Chinese Communist Party, 1921–72*, Praeger, New York, 1973.

He Jingzhi, Ding Yi and Ma Ke, *Geju Baimao nü xuanqu* (*Selections from the opera* The White-Haired Girl), China Record Press, Beijing, 1964.

Hinton, William, *Fanshen: A Documentary of Revolution in a Chinese Village*, Monthly Review Press, New York, 1966.

Hsiung, James C. and Steven I. Levine (eds), *China's Bitter Victory: The War with Japan 1937–1945*, M. E. Sharpe, Armonk, New York and London 1992.

Hsü, Immanuel C. Y., *The Rise of Modern China*, 5th edn, Oxford University Press, New York, 1995.

Israel, John, *Student Nationalism in China, 1927–1937*, Stanford University Press, Stanford, 1966.

Johnson, Chalmers A., *Peasant Nationalism and Communist Power: The Emergence of Revolutionary China 1937–1945*, Stanford University Press, Stanford, 1962.

Johnston, Reginald F., *Twilight in the Forbidden City*, Victor Gollancz, London, 1934; Oxford University Press, Hong Kong, Oxford and New York, 1985.

Keating, Pauline, *Two Revolutions: Village Reconstruction and the Cooperative Movement in Northern Shaanxi, 1934–1945*, Stanford University Press, Stanford, 1997.

Knight, Nick, *Li Da and Marxist Philosophy in China*, Westview, Boulder, Colorado, 1996.

Knight, Nick, *Rethinking Mao: Explorations in Mao Zedong's Thought*, Rowman & Littlefield, Lanham, 2007.

Kwei Chungshu (ed.), *The Chinese Year Book*, 7 vols premier issue 1935–6, final issue 1944–5, Shanghai, Kraus Reprint, Nendeln/Liechtenstein, 1968.

Lang, Olga, *Chinese Family and Society*, Yale University Press, New Haven, 1946.

Lary, Diana, *China's Republic*, Cambridge University Press, Cambridge and New York, 2007.

Lee, Leo Ou-fan, *Voices from the Iron House: A Study of Lu Xun*, Indiana University Press, Bloomington, 1987.

Leiter, Samuel L., *Encyclopedia of Asian Theatre*, Greenwood Press, Westport, Connecticut, and London, 2007.

Levine, Steven, *Anvil of Victory: The Communist Revolution in Manchuria, 1945–1948*, Columbia University Press, New York, 1987.

Li, Lincoln, *Student Nationalism in China, 1924–49*, State University of New York Press, Albany, 1994.

Liang Qichao, *Yinbing shi quanji (Complete Works of Liang Qichao)*, 48 vols, China Bookshop, Shanghai, 1916.

Lin Yutang, *My Country and my People*, John Day, New York, 1935.

Lin Yutang, *The Importance of Living*, Readers Union, by arrangement with William Heinemann, London, 1939.

Mackerras, Colin, *The Chinese Theatre in Modern Times, From 1840 to the Present Day*, Thames & Hudson, London, 1975.

Mackerras, Colin, *Western Images of China*, Oxford University Press, Hong Kong, 1989.

Mackerras, Colin, with the assistance of Robert Chan, *Modern China: A Chronology from 1842 to the Present*, Thames & Hudson, London, 1982.

Mackerras, Colin and Amanda Yorke, *The Cambridge Handbook of Contemporary China*, Cambridge University Press, Cambridge, 1991.

Mao Tse-tung [Zedong], *Selected Works of Mao Tse-tung*, vols I to V, Foreign Languages Press, Peking, 1965–77.

Mao Tse-tung [Zedong], 'The great union of the popular masses', trans. Stuart R. Schram, *The China Quarterly*, no. 49, January/March 1972, 76–87.

Marsh, Robert M., *The Mandarins: The Circulation of Elites in China, 1600–1900*, The Free Press of Glencoe, New York, 1961.

Martin, Bernard, *Strange Vigour: A Biography of Sun Yat-sen*, William Heinemann, London, 1944.

McAleavy, Henry, *The Modern History of China*, Weidenfeld & Nicolson, London, 1967.

McCord, Edward A., *The Power of the Gun: The Emergence of Modern Chinese Warlordism*, University of California Press, Berkeley, 1993.

McCormack, Gavan, *Chang Tso-lin in Northeast China, 1911–1928: China, Japan, China and the Manchurian Idea*, Stanford University Press, Stanford, Dawson, and Folkestone, 1977.

McDougall, Bonnie S. and Kam Louie, *The Literature of China in the Twentieth Century*, C. Hurst & Co., London, 1997; Bushbooks, Gosford, New South Wales, 1998.

Meisner, Maurice, *Li Ta-chao and the Origins of Chinese Marxism*, Harvard University Press, Cambridge, Mass., 1967.

Melby, John F., *The Mandate of Heaven: Record of a Civil War, China 1945–49*, University of Toronto Press, Toronto, 1968; Chatto & Windus, London, 1969.

Moise, Edwin E., *Modern China: A History*, 2nd edn, Longman, Harlow, Essex, 1994.

Morse, Hosea Ballou, *The International Relations of the Chinese Empire*, 3 vols, first published 1910–18; Paragon Book Gallery, New York, 1971.

Payne, Robert, *Mao Tse-tung*, Schuman, New York, 1950.

Pepper, Suzanne, *Civil War in China: The Political Struggle, 1945–1949*, University of California Press, Berkeley, 1978.

Pepper, Suzanne, 'The political odyssey of an intellectual construct: peasant nationalism and the study of China's revolutionary history – a review essay', *The Journal of Asian Studies*, vol. 63, no. 1, February 2004, 105–25.

Phillips, Richard T., *China Since 1911*, Macmillan, Basingstoke, 1966.

Pomeranz, Kenneth, *The Making of a Hinterland: State, Society and Economy in Inland North China, 1853–1937*, University of California Press, Berkeley, 1993.

Pong, David and Edmund S. K. Fung (eds), *Ideal and Reality: Social and Political Change in Modern China 1860–1949*, University Press of America, Lanham, 1985.

Porter, Robin, *Industrial Reformers in Republican China*, M. E. Sharpe, Armonk, 1994.

Pye, Lucian W., *Warlord Politics: Conflict and Coalition in the Modernization of Republican China*, Praeger, New York, 1971.

Research Room of the Chinese Communist Party Central Committee's Editorial and Translation Bureau for the Works of Marx, Engels, Lenin and Stalin, comp., *Wusi shiqi qikan jieshao (diyi ji)* (*An Introduction to the Periodicals of the May Fourth Period*) (vol. I), People's Press, Beijing, 1958.

Rhoads, Edward J. M., *Manchu and Han: Ethnic Relations and Political Power in Late Qing and Early Republican China, 1861–1928*, University of Washington Press, Seattle and London, 2000.

Rigby, Richard W., *The May 30 Movement: Events and Themes*, Australian National University Press, Canberra, 1980.

Rue, John E., *Mao Tse-tung in Opposition, 1927–1935*, Stanford University Press, Stanford, 1966.

Saich, Tony, *The Origins of the First United Front in China: The Role of Sneevliet (Alias Maring)*, 2 vols, Brill, Leiden, 1991.

Saich, Tony (ed.), *The Rise to Power of the Chinese Communist Party: Documents and Analysis*, with a contribution by Benjamin Yang, M. E. Sharpe, New York, 1996.

Saich, Tony and Hans van de Ven (eds), *New Perspectives on the Chinese Communist Revolution*, M. E. Sharpe, Armonk, 1995.

Schiffrin, Harold Z., *Sun Yat-sen and the Origins of the Chinese Revolution*, University of California Press, 1968.

Schiffrin, Harold Z., *Sun Yat-sen, Reluctant Revolutionary*, Little, Brown and Company, Boston and Toronto, 1980.

Schram, Stuart R., *Mao Tse-tung*, Penguin, Harmondsworth, 1966.

Schram, Stuart R., *The Political Thought of Mao Tse-tung*, Frederick A. Praeger, New York, 1963; revised and enlarged edition Penguin, Harmondsworth, and Praeger, New York, 1969.

Schwarcz, Vera, *Chinese Enlightenment: Intellectuals and the Legacy of the May Fourth Movement of 1919*, University of California Press, Berkeley, 1986.

Schwartz, Benjamin, *Chinese Communism and the Rise of Mao*, Harvard University Press, Cambridge, Mass., 1951.

Selden, Mark, *The Yenan Way in Revolutionary China*, Harvard University Press, Cambridge, 1971.

Selden, Mark, *China in Revolution: The Yenan Way Revisited*, M. E. Sharpe, Armonk, 1995.

Sheridan, James E., *Chinese Warlord: The Career of Feng Yü-hsiang*, Stanford University Press, Stanford, 1966.

Sheridan, James E., *China in Disintegration: The Republican Era in Chinese History, 1912–1949*, Free Press, New York, and Collier Macmillan, London, 1975.

Short, Philip, *Mao, A Life*, Hodder & Stoughton, London, 1999; Henry Holt, New York, 2000.

Sills, David L. (ed.), *International Encyclopedia of the Social Sciences*, 18 vols, Macmillan and Free Press, New York, 1968, 1972.

Siu, Bobby, *Women of China, Imperialism and Women's Resistance 1900–1949*, Zed Press, London, 1982.

Snow, Edgar, *Red Star Over China*, Victor Gollancz, London, 1937; Penguin, Harmondsworth, 1972.

Snow, Helen Foster, *Women in Modern China*, Mouton & Co, The Hague and Paris, 1967.

Spence, Jonathan D., *The Search for Modern China*, W. W. Norton & Company, New York, London, 1990.

Sun Shuyun, *The Long March*, HarperCollins, 2006.

Sun Yat-sen, *San Min Chu I, The Three Principles of the People*, trans. Frank W. Price, ed. L. T. Chen, The Commercial Press, Shanghai, 1927.

Sun Yat-sen, *Guofu quanji* (*Complete Works of the Father of the Nation*), 6 vols, Chinese Nationalist Party Central Committee Historical Material on Party History Committee, Taibei, 1973, 1981.

Tang Tao (ed.), *History of Modern Chinese Literature*, Foreign Languages Press, Beijing, 1993.

Teiwes, Frederick C. with Warren Sun, *The Formation of the Maoist Leadership: From the Return of Wang Ming to the Seventh Party Congress*, Contemporary China Institute, London, 1994.

Terrill, Ross, *Mao, A Biography*, Hale & Iremonger, Sydney, 1995.

Thompson, Peter and Robert Macklin, *The Man Who Died Twice: The Life and Adventures of Morrison of Peking*, Allen & Unwin, Sydney, 2004.

Trapido, Joel (ed.), *An International Dictionary of Theatre Language*, Greenwood Press, Westport, Connecticut, and London, 1985.

Tsou Jung [Zou Rong], *The Revolutionary Army: A Chinese Nationalist Tract of 1903*, introduction and translation with notes by John Lust, Matériaux pour l'étude de l'Extrême-orient moderne et contemporain, Textes 6, Mouton & Co., The Hague and Paris, 1968.

van de Ven, Hans J., *From Friend to Comrade: The Founding of the Chinese Communist Party, 1920–1927*, University of California Press, Berkeley, 1991.

Waldron, Arthur, *From War to Nationalism: China's Turning Point, 1924–1925*, Cambridge University Press, Cambridge, 1995.

Wang Niankun, *Xuesheng yundong shiyao jianghua* (*Speeches from the History of the Student Movement*), Shangza Press, Shanghai, 1951.

Wang Zheng, *Women in the Chinese Enlightenment: Oral and Textual Histories*, University of California Press, Berkeley, Los Angeles, London, 1999.

Welch, Holmes, *The Buddhist Revival in China*, Harvard University Press, Cambridge, Mass., 1968.

White, Theodore H. and Annalee Jacoby, *Thunder out of China*, William Sloane Associates, New York, 1946.

Wilbur, C. Martin, *Sun Yat-sen, Frustrated Patriot*, Columbia University Press, New York, 1976.

Wilbur, C. Martin, *The Nationalist Revolution in China, 1923–1928*, Cambridge University Press, Cambridge, 1984.

Wilbur, C. Martin (ed.), with introductory essays by C. Martin Wilbur and Julie Lien-ying How, *Documents on Commission, Nationalism, and Soviet Advisers in China 1918–1927*, Columbia University Press, New York, 1956.

Wilson, Dick, *The Long March, 1935: The Epic of Chinese Communism's Survival*, Viking, New York, 1971.

Wilson, Dick (ed.), *Mao Tse-tung in the Scales of History: A Preliminary Assessment Organized by The China Quarterly*, Cambridge University Press, Cambridge, 1977.

Woodhead, H. G. W. and H. T. M. Bell (comp.), *The China Year Book*, 20 vols, G. Routledge, London, 1912–19; Tientsin Press, Tientsin, 1921–30; The North China Daily News & Herald, Shanghai, 1931–39.

Wou, Odoric Y. K., *Militarism in Modern China: The Career of Wu P'ei-Fu, 1916–39*, Dawson, Folkstone, and Australian National University Press, Canberra, 1978.

Wou, Odoric Y. K., *Mobilizing the Masses: Building Revolution in Henan*, Stanford University Press, Stanford, 1994.

Wright, Mary C. (ed.), *China in Revolution: The First Phase, 1900–1913*, Yale University Press, New Haven, 1968.

Wright, Tim, *Coal Mining in China's Economy and Society, 1895–1937*, Cambridge University Press, Cambridge, 1984.

Wright, Tim (ed.), *The Chinese Economy in the Early Twentieth Century: Recent Chinese Studies*, St Martin's Press, New York, 1992.

Xu Zhigeng, *Lest We Forget: Nanjing Massacre, 1937*, trans. Zhang Tingquan and Lin Wusun, ed. Lin Wusun, Panda Books, Chinese Literature Press, 1995.

Young, Ernest P., *The Presidency of Yuan Shih-k'ai: Liberalism and Dictatorship in Early Republican China*, University of Michigan Press, Ann Arbor, 1977.

Zhao Suisheng, *Power by Design: Constitution-Making in Nationalist China*, University of Hawai'i Press, Honolulu, 1996.

Zhongguo xin wenxue daxi (*Compendium of New Chinese Literature*), 10 vols, Hong Kong Literature Press, Hong Kong, n.d.

Index